"For a comprehensive guide on taking a strategic approach to making the best use of LinkedIn, Sandra Long's book, *LinkedIn for Personal Branding*, is the ticket! Among the many resources on LinkedIn, Ms. Long's book stands out. Her book provides a readable, approachable guide to not only addressing the nuts and bolts of creating an effective profile, but also addressing how to think about yourself as a marketable brand and utilize LinkedIn to get your brand noticed. I particularly appreciate the stories, examples, and facts sprinkled throughout. *LinkedIn for Personal Branding* will be a 'go-to' resource I'll use when referring career-seeking working professionals to valuable career tools!"

Laurie Sedgwick
Director of Career Management,
Executive MBA Programs, and
Alumni Support
Johnson School @ Cornell
University

"Sandra's book, *LinkedIn for Personal Branding*, is unique because it provides a *strategic* perspective on personal branding as it applies to the LinkedIn profile and thought leadership. It's loaded with easy tips and practical examples. A must-read for anyone trying to improve their online image."

Mary Abbazia
Coauthor of *The Accidental Marketer*

"LinkedIn is the foundation of every professional's personal brand. Sandra Long provides you with a formula for success to grow, enhance and expand your business and professional network for every person in every profession. Pick up a copy of her book to take your personal brand to the next level on LinkedIn."

Jessica Miller-Merrell
Founder of Blogging4Jobs and
Workology
Author of *Tweet This! Twitter for Business*

"Sandra Long promises to help you create and manage your personal brand on LinkedIn, and she delivers! Her attention to detail, specific tips, examples, and recommendations help you craft an authentic and powerful LinkedIn profile for your professional success. This is truly the 'ultimate guide' for personal branding on LinkedIn and is perfect for anyone just beginning social selling or looking to increase their exposure and thought leadership."

Bonnie Marcus
Author of *Politics of Promotion:
How High Achieving Women Get
Ahead and Stay Ahead*

LinkedIn™ for Personal Branding: The Ultimate Guide

By Sandra Long

Published by
Hybrid Global Publishing
355 Lexington Avenue
New York, NY 10017

Manufactured in the United States of America, or in the United Kingdom when distributed elsewhere.

Author: Long, Sandra
    Title: LinkedIn For Personal Branding: The Ultimate Guide
    ISBN:
    Paperback: 9781938015434
    eBook: 9781938015441

Cover design by: Joe Potter
Interior design: Scribe Inc.

Author's URL: http://www.linkedinforpersonalbranding.com

CONTENTS

ACKNOWLEDGMENTS

Warm thank-yous and appreciation to my very supportive clients, partners, friends, and family. I have to say that I am a most fortunate person. In particular, warm thank-yous need to be extended to the following:

- My advance book readers: Mary Abbazia, Barbara Hannan, Bryan Mattimore, Tom Long, Andrew Long, and Jessica Long. All of you were so helpful, reading my chapters and book and providing valuable input and ideas.
- The wonderful clients and friends who allowed me to share their stories and/or profiles in this book. This includes Felix Giannini, Lynn Garelick, Lisa Bonner, Amy Krompinger, Craig Flaherty, Marie Patel, Jorge Periera, Emily Chalk, Mark Ehrenzeller, Aneta Hall, Lisa Bernard, Dave Czarneski, Bonnie Marcus, Mary Abbazzia, Thomas Spitale, Valerie Senew, Steve Gardiner, Bryan Mattimore, Jennifer Buchholz, Mary Beth Moran Nelsen, and Kathy McShane.
- The many clients who inspired me including Bob Ageloff, Drew Saunders, Paul Lewis, Bart Casabona, Mary Lang, Jim Daly, and many more.
- The dedicated and talented team at Post Road Consulting LLC including Heather Salvatore, Craig Patton, and Jacqui Nichols. You make working much more fun!
- The educators, continuing-education leaders, and university professors and administrators that I have had the pleasure of working with.
- All writers and authors, for which I have the utmost admiration. I never understood how hard and long the book writing process is.
- My publishing team at HG Publishing, headed by Karen Strauss. I appreciate the expertise and hard work from the whole team.
- And most of all, my immediate family Tom, Andrew, and Jessica—all of whom I adore—along with their mates Jacqui and Andrew and of course sweet little Joseph. My incredibly wonderful parents, Richard and Betty Gustafson, deserve a huge round of applause for helping me all of my life. You are all loved, adored, and appreciated.

INTRODUCTION

I was always "the new girl" while growing up. My family moved across state lines several times but always in the northeastern United States. As an older child and a teenager, I remember thinking that I could start fresh by creating a positive impression as I entered a new neighborhood or school. It wasn't hard to do. I was always starting over, and I realized it was an opportunity more than a problem. Those childhood first impressions began in the classroom, playground, or neighborhood.

Some things about being new stick with you forever. I was teased for a Boston accent (which I no longer have) in upstate New York and for my attire (which I quickly adjusted) in Pennsylvania. First impressions are developed immediately, and that has not changed. Whether you are starting over or not, you still have the opportunity to shape others opinions of you and your capabilities.

Branding was a word reserved for products or companies. Now it's becoming a part of our vocabulary. Personal branding is not just for celebrities anymore. It's a phrase that has accelerated in popularity with blogging, social media, and, especially, LinkedIn, from a professional perspective.

Some people don't like the phrase "personal branding," perhaps because they think it seems pretentious. However, I am finding more and more people using the phrase. In a 2016 survey conducted by Post Road Consulting, 43 percent of the respondents have been aware of their personal brand for over three years.

We are each known for something, and we can choose to demonstrate and manage our brand to enhance our professional opportunities. Your personal brand is what makes you unique as an employee, leader, partner, speaker, or entrepreneur.

If you ignore your personal brand, it will be shaped entirely by others. Your personal brand is already out there, but is it firmly in your control?

Your brand includes a combination of your reputation, what people say about you, what you say about yourself, and what they find online. Do nothing and you might be OK, but you forfeit the opportunity to frame the opinions that others have of you.

Consider

Do you really think your network will remember the amazing project or article from three years ago without the help of your LinkedIn profile? Don't take that chance. Other people focus on their brand, probably not yours.

Growing up, we did use the word "reputation." As a girl, this was always an important word because every girl wanted to have a sterling reputation. I remember going into the work world and still caring about reputation. At that point, I worked in sales in a mostly male environment. So I wanted to be known as very professional and hardworking. I always wore very conservative clothes and tried to work harder than anyone else on the sales team. Looking back, I think it paid off for me.

Today a good portion of our reputation or personal brand is established online, oftentimes before we walk in the door or reach for the phone. Assume that your contacts are researching you on both Google and LinkedIn. That first impression is created from your LinkedIn profile and any other hits from a Google search. This evaluation of you happens before and after sales meetings or interviews.

"Interestingly, 65% of people agree that the impression you make online is just as important as the one you make in person."

LinkedIn, May 26, 2016

The good news is that you can easily create an online presence that genuinely reflects your personal brand using LinkedIn. This will help you impress potential clients, partners, colleagues, community members, and hiring managers.

People are looking online for everyone. They are looking for you in advance of a meeting or interview. They are checking out your profile page after your presentation. Most likely, the first impression people have of you will be as a result of their digital research. First impressions are now made on LinkedIn!

This book reflects my opinions and perspective. It's the advice I share in my classes and speeches and with clients. I have learned a lot from all the workshops and my various students over the past few years. My company, Post Road Consulting, has also conducted a LinkedIn and personal branding survey that will be referred to in this book.

Different consultants and experts may look at LinkedIn and personal branding in a different way and that is certainly OK. In fact, we all learn from each other. I believe that we all evolve in our thinking too. Decide for yourself what is the best path for you.

Expect change. Your personal brand should be evolving. On top of that, expect LinkedIn to add, modify, or remove features. Therefore, I plan to revise this book regularly, but remember your responsibility to keep up your own brand and profile.

My intention is for this book to be more about creating your unique personal branding strategy using LinkedIn rather than sharing every specific "how to" on a LinkedIn profile, which you can easily find elsewhere. For that reason, I have developed a companion website with all the applicable links for you. Find the list of "how to" resources at the end of each chapter. I will work hard to keep these updated.

The personal branding principles in this book may also apply to Facebook or other channels, but our focus for this book is strictly LinkedIn.

There are other excellent resources regarding both LinkedIn and personal branding, but I wanted this book to be about the strategy of *considering them together*. Here's my promise for every reader: you will learn how to create and manage your personal brand using LinkedIn.

You will learn how to be found online and how to manage a compelling and authentic personal brand on LinkedIn. This is not about creating something that is not truly you, but about expressing the real you, the best you, online. At Post Road Consulting, we developed our own system to achieve this called True North Personal Branding^{SM}.

Read this book in whatever order works for you. However, it has been arranged in a logical flow. We'll cover personal branding first, then overarching topics such as keywords and images, and then the various sections of the profile. We'll finish with four chapters about "thought leadership." Please note that the appendices are also here to help you, so don't miss those.

I am excited to get started on this journey with you! In the following chapters, we will go step-by-step together as you learn about all the ways to incorporate your most compelling personal brand elements into your LinkedIn profile, and we will go further by exploring how you can leverage the thought leadership opportunities of LinkedIn.

You will notice that this book includes a few stories and screenshots of real people who created an online personal brand on LinkedIn to advance their business or career opportunities. I appreciate being able to refer to these example profiles, which should make the theories and ideas more accessible.

You can demonstrate and manage your own brand online very easily. You will soon see how it will help you advance your career and business opportunities. I assure you that it will be very satisfying and worth the effort!

You and Your Brand

CHAPTER 1

Your LinkedIn Opportunities

I have learned that many people are frustrated and confused about LinkedIn. Some are nervous and unsure about being online. I've had people come into my workshops sharing their concerns. Primarily, my customers and friends are worried about opportunities they are missing if they're not on LinkedIn or if their profile isn't up to par.

Missed LinkedIn opportunities fall into the categories of career, sales, business development, speaking, and networking, and they also include missed opportunities to develop industry recognition and connections. Opportunities are missed every day, every hour, and every minute. Don't let that be you.

Let's start by examining career opportunities. It's well known that recruiters and hiring managers are searching for candidates on the LinkedIn platform. Make sure your profile is optimized for search so that you can always be easily found. Simply follow the advice in this book, and you are on your way to being found. At a bare minimum, you should have a 100 percent complete profile as described in chapter 3.

What about referred candidates who may be either passively or actively looking for a new position? Hiring managers and recruiters are also looking at those profiles every day too. Most employers will research your name as soon as someone mentions it or refers you. If he or she were impressed during an interview, the employer will likely be reviewing your LinkedIn profile to validate things and dig deeper.

Flip this coin to the other side. Consider the personal brand of recruiters and hiring managers. Today's candidates want to know about the recruiter and hiring manager. Your personal brand as demonstrated on LinkedIn can cause a reaction from those you are trying to recruit. Is this the right reaction? Is this a nonreaction? You have the opportunity to share your personal philosophy and why it's great to work at your company. These things matter to candidates, especially for Millennials.

Sales and business development has changed forever. Think about it, buyers have changed drastically. Fewer and fewer buyers accept a cold call or react positively to old-fashioned telemarketing efforts. Buyers want to work with a trusted resource, probably someone who has been referred directly to them from a friend or colleague. Buyers will research the company and look for the industry experts well before they will engage with a salesperson or consultant.

According to LinkedIn, 90 percent of decision makers never answer a cold call from a salesperson. Today's executives want to be referred. LinkedIn states that 76 percent of B2B buyers prefer vendors referred by people they know. Once referred, it is often common practice to look at a LinkedIn profile for validation.

Buyers have changed how they research companies' products, services, and sellers before they even engage with a conversation. The best salespeople have to position themselves, their company, and their expertise in order to attract clients, and this is still true even after a warm referral. Salespeople and consultants have to consider their personal brand along with their company brand and how that all syncs together. Personal and company branding is the first step of a social selling, social recruiting, or social job search initiative.

Sandra's Definitions (Notice the Similarities)

Social selling is the ability to find, engage, connect with, and attract buyers using social media in order to create or advance a sales opportunity pipeline. Social selling incorporates personal branding, thought leadership, prospecting, and relationship building to position the salesperson more favorably with today's buyers.

Social recruiting is the ability to find, engage, connect with, and attract candidates using social media in order to create or advance a talent pipeline. Social recruiting incorporates personal branding, thought leadership, prospecting, and relationship building to position the recruiter more favorably with today's candidates.

Social job search is the ability to find, engage, connect with, and attract employers and recruiters using social media in order to create or advance career opportunities. Social job search incorporates personal branding, thought leadership, prospecting, and relationship building to position the job searcher more favorably with today's employers.

Social buying is the ability to find, engage, and connect with professional contacts to make informed purchasing decisions leveraging relationships, referrals, and knowledge gathering from social media. Social buyers are self-directed knowledge seekers who value genuine expertise and relationships. Today's social buyers are finding marketplace advantages for themselves, their company or organization by using social media.

Your LinkedIn profile is your best opportunity to presell yourself for any professional opportunity.

Albert's Story

Your personal brand will impact how often you are being referred. One of my clients is an attorney who told me that he was missing major referral opportunities. His friend was hesitant about referring him until he had a professional LinkedIn profile. This was a missed opportunity. Once Albert updated his personal brand and profile on LinkedIn, he was quickly introduced to new prospective clients.

For salespeople, attorneys, consultants, or executives, this is a lot to consider. In addition to a professional personal brand that is in sync with your firm, you will want to know how to effectively and efficiently use LinkedIn for prospecting and networking. For company leaders, you need to consider the tools and training that your team will need to be successful.

Thought leadership is the new marketing. Consider sharing your expertise to open up new industry opportunities. If you're collaborating within your industry or want to become known as an expert, as a thought leader, or as a speaker, then LinkedIn is very important to you as well. Your colleagues will be searching for your profile before meeting you or hearing you speak. We'll be diving deeper into thought leadership in chapters 14 through 17.

Whether it's premeeting research, finding industry association leaders, or connecting with event planners and other corporate decision makers, LinkedIn is very important for any of us that want to be considered experts in a particular industry or field. Speakers, authors, and experts of all kinds are using LinkedIn to establish a great online presence.

Evolve

A personal brand should not be a static situation. It is truly something that evolves over time. Many of us are transitioning from the corporate world to become entrepreneurs and certainly need help with a professional online brand. Stay-at-home parents are transitioning to a new professional world where online profiles are the standard. College students are asking their universities to teach them the best practices for LinkedIn so that they can have a great start to building a professional brand and network.

No matter who we are as professionals, our mission is to portray an image that is truthful and authentic and reflects who we are and the unique professional value that we can deliver. We are truly all works in progress, and it never stops. So don't think you ever really "finish" your LinkedIn profile!

In this book, I will share many real-life stories and screenshot examples of some of my friends and clients. If you invest your time to perfect your brand, then others will see you in a different light. You'll be surprised at the reaction, which should include referrals and introductions. And those should turn into sales, career, and industry opportunities.

I am fortunate that many sales and speaking opportunities came to me as a result of my activity and presence on LinkedIn. Many of my clients either found me on LinkedIn or heard my name and then checked out my profile. I can usually tell that a prospect is interested in advance because I can see him or her looking at my profile on the popular "Who's Viewed Your Profile" page. This was happening to me well before I became a LinkedIn trainer and speaker.

LinkedIn Landscape

Available in 24 languages
35 percent of users access LinkedIn every day
45 million profiles are viewed on LinkedIn every day
430 million users globally, with 2 new users joining every second

Read this book and then commit to sharing your own genuine personal brand online using LinkedIn. Before you begin, I ask that you consider creating goals and think about your audience. Who will be reading your profile page? And what do you want to have happened as a result of him or her reading your profile?

Your industry reputation will also impact your career and sales opportunities, right? In my classes, I always say that folks are either "job seekers" or "salespeople," and really they are the same thing! If you are happily employed and not looking for a job, that's OK too, but don't fool yourself. You should always be a salesperson and recruiter for your company and a job seeker for yourself.

TIP: Envision the people who will be viewing your LinkedIn Profile in advance.

Let's review the benefits of using LinkedIn for your personal branding:

1. Increased sales, recruiting, or consulting opportunities
2. Acceleration of your career
3. Increased speaking or teaching opportunities
4. Leadership opportunities
5. Partnering opportunities
6. Enhanced credibility and name recognition

It all works together if you are focused on your personal brand. Using LinkedIn for personal branding is the best way to make professional opportunities a reality.

CHAPTER 2

Your Personal Brand and Your Best Authentic Self

Personal branding is actively managing your image and defining your unique value. If you don't take this action, no one else is likely to do it.

You may have heard about the concept of "creating a personal brand," but in all reality, you want to be true to yourself, your skills, and your personality. It's more about showing or demonstrating your best genuine self than creating anything totally new. You don't want to be creating a false impression or presence.

Everything needs to be true about yourself, but you can certainly work to share the best you. Can you imagine if someone were to create a phony online presence that doesn't match the real person? It just does not work. Ever.

Dr. Seuss wrote dozens of wonderful books, many with personal branding quotes or themes. Dr. Seuss said: "Today You are You, that is Truer than True. There is no one alive who is Youer than You."

So just what is personal branding?

Tom Peters wrote "The Brand Called You" in 1997 for *Fast Company*. Peters says: "We are CEO's of our own companies: Me Inc. To be in business today, our most important job is to be head marketer for the brand called You." Mr. Peters was ahead of his time. Now, years later, the personal branding revolution is going full steam ahead.

In addition to experience and skills, personal branding may incorporate *your personality, passion, drivers, values, and your vision*. Your brand will vary depending on what's most important to you. Do you know any of these people? Notice that they are all more than a job or title:

- Honest Abe—a realtor
- Helpful Helen—an insurance consultant
- Networked Ned—a recruiter

- Wendy, the woman who never gives up. Ever!—an inside sales rep
- Sam, who started over from scratch—an entrepreneur
- Ann, who overcame adversity—an author and speaker
- Creative Carl—a digital marketing expert

Your personal brand may include many of the more "intangible" aspects in addition to your experience and skills. Think about yourself: What are the unique qualities that express your values and self? Do any of these phrases apply to you?

- I am a problem solver.
- I am a continuous learner.
- I never give up.
- I transformed myself, or I am transforming myself now.
- I am starting over.
- I put others ahead of myself.
- I followed my heart.
- I aim high.
- I am creative.
- I treat others the way I want to be treated.
- I hold myself accountable.
- I make a difference.
- I am grateful.
- I am a survivor.
- I am an optimist.
- I trust my instincts.
- I overcome obstacles.
- I am a straight shooter.
- I have the courage to be honest.
- I value loyalty.
- I understand the importance or value of time, relationships, teamwork, or . . .
- I have learned that . . .

Your brand is demonstrated in many ways and places. Think about all the factors that impact other people's impressions of you as a professional. Your brand attributes can be found across the following:

Online	Offline	Hard Copy and Digital
websites	attire	business cards
anything about you from Google Search	attitude and network body language (e.g., smiles and handshakes)	brochures or sell sheets company overviews
blog posts		proposals
LinkedIn profiles	sales meetings	resumes or CVs
Facebook, Twitter, or other social profiles	career fairs presentations	cover letters biographies
social media posts	candidate meetings	presentations and speeches
social media messaging	new hire onboarding	videos
e-mail messages	meetings	audio podcasts or radio
Wikipedia pages	board meetings	letters
Amazon or other author pages	meet-ups interviews	your attitude and network projects and roles
biographies on company websites	what people say about you	recommendations, reviews, endorsements your own book(s)

This book focuses strictly on using LinkedIn to establish and enhance your personal brand image and thought leadership. It's a good idea to consider all of the other ways to display the key elements of your brand—and be consistent with your LinkedIn profile.

> **Question 1:** What are strategic elements from the list above that you may want to add to your LinkedIn profile and use to represent your brand?
>
> **Question 2:** Which items have words, images, or ideas that you wish to integrate into your profile and personal brand?
>
> **Question 3:** Which of these items (in addition to your LinkedIn profile) do you need to edit or update?

Personal Brand Elements on the LinkedIn Profile

The chart below shows several possible attributes of a personal brand on the left side, with suggestions of where in a LinkedIn profile there is an appropriate place to demonstrate those attributes.

Personal brand attributes	LinkedIn profile sections—partial list
Experience	Experience, Organization, Volunteering, Publications, Certifications, Patents, Summary, Headline, LinkedIn Publisher Posts, Rich Media, Interests
Skills	Skills, Experience, Volunteering, Organizations, Summary, Rich Media, Interests
Learning	Education, Certifications, Courses, Summary, LinkedIn Publisher Posts
Goals	Summary, LinkedIn Publisher Posts, Rich Media, Advice for Contacting, Interests, Headline

Personal brand attributes	LinkedIn profile sections—partial list
Reputation	Recommendations, Endorsements, Rich Media
Passion	Summary, interests, Volunteering, Publications, Rich Media, Headline
Values	Volunteering, Interests, Publications, Summary, LinkedIn Publisher Posts, Rich Media, Interests
Personality	Interests, Summary, LinkedIn Publisher Posts, Rich Media, Advice for Contacting
Your story	Summary, Publications, LinkedIn Publisher Posts, Rich Media
Network and community	Organizations, Volunteering, Groups, Projects, Connections, Recommendations, Endorsements
Vision	Summary, Publications, LinkedIn Publisher Posts, Rich Media, Headline
Presence and attitude	Summary, Recommendations, Rich Media, Publications, LinkedIn Publisher Posts
Trust and proof	Recommendations, Endorsements, Projects, Images, Publications, LinkedIn Publisher Posts, Rich Media
Interests	Interests, Summary, Volunteering, Rich Media
Leadership and mindshare	Summary, Volunteering, Experience, Projects, Publications, LinkedIn Publisher Posts, Rich Media, Recommendations
Engagement, sharing, and etiquette	Recommendations, Projects, Endorsements, Status updates, Comments, Posts
Unique value	Headline, Summary

The specific elements most applicable to you can be prioritized. Then you can communicate your unique value by sharing a story or an example.

TIP: Start with your brand elements. Determine which LinkedIn sections are the best fit.

Case Study: Lynn Garelick of Greenwich, Connecticut

Lynn Garelick is an interior designer and business owner working in Fairfield County, Connecticut, and New York City. Her personal brand as expressed on LinkedIn has these attributes:

Lynn's personal brand elements	LinkedIn profile sections
Experience and skills: Owner and interior designer Connecticut and New York	Experience, Skills, Projects, Summary, and Images (professional portfolio)
Passion and interests: Art, history, gardens	Interests, Organizations, Volunteering, Projects
Values, personality, and story: Helpful, grateful, customer oriented	Summary, Volunteering, Organizations

Example One

Lynn Garelick's images from her profile help us visualize her work and are a testimony to her talent:

Purchase NY Showhouse Master Suite   Purchase NY Showhouse Master Suite

NYC - Living Room   NYC - Living room   NYC - Living/Dining Area

Example Two

Lynn Garelick's Volunteering section (shown below) is a wonderful demonstration of some of her passions and interests. In addition, Lynn displays "organizations" in her profile that show her passion for art, history, gardens, and the community. Lynn is much more than a talented designer. She demonstrates deep commitment and passion in her community.

 Volunteer Experience & Causes

Church Historian, Property Committee
Christ Church Greenwich CT

I have been a member of Christ Episcopal Church in Greenwich CT, 1999 to the present. I researched and created the Christ Church Historical Timeline. As historian, I also respond to all inquiries relating to past parishioners or events.
I have also been a member of the Property Commission for the past 15 years; the committee is responsible for all maintenance issues for the properties of the church.

Docent
Bruce Museum, Greenwich CT

As a docent volunteer, I conduct tours of all of the art shows at the museum,

Committee Member
League of Women Voters, Greenwich CT Chapter

Oral History Project Interviewer
Greenwich Public Library
January 2016 – Present (4 months) | Education

Lynn's Organizations

 Organizations

ASID - American Society of Interior Designers- Connecticut Chapter
Professional Member and President 2012-2013

NCIDQ -National Council of Interior Designers
Professional Member

Greenwich Arts Council
Board Member and Secretary

American Pen Women
Member
Starting 2010

Greenwich Art Society
Member/artist

Art Society of Old Greenwich
Member/artist

The Carriage Barn Art Society, New Canaan CT
Member/artist

Live Your Brand

Be an amazing brand. Know your strengths. Build it out and demonstrate it. Being successful on LinkedIn is not only about being successful online. Your online presence needs to work together with what you are doing in the real world. So if you are an expert in something, make sure you are sharing it, writing about it, speaking about it, or helping others. Much of the work that you do is a great demonstration and validation of your strengths. It is up to you to be an amazing brand, to differentiate yourself and become memorable.

Start by thinking about yourself. Do you let people see the real you? What are you known for? What do people say about you? Have you asked people what they think you are exceptionally good at? How would your friends and colleagues describe you as a person?

And what do you want to be known for? Becoming known for something is not just about putting it online. When you want to become known for something, you need to take action to demonstrate that those are your skills, expertise, or values. It needs to become a part of your life. If you want to be known for being honest, don't just put that value statement on LinkedIn. Make sure you are living honestly every day. Make sure that your life matches your online brand!

If you want to be known as a subject matter expert, what are you doing in real life to demonstrate that? Don't just talk about it, be sure to show it and share it! So it might make sense to speak, write, publish, teach, or mentor other people about your topic to become known for your topic. During this process of teaching or speaking, you will find that your expertise will grow.

Being a writer, mentor, or a speaker will also mean you are a continuous learner. Set up a Google Alert on your specific topic so you are reading the latest news every day. Join online communities that focus on your topic. You will learn even more from your readers, students, audiences, competitors, and customers.

Your personal brand and your expertise will grow as you speak and write. Of course, your writing, mentoring, or speaking should be featured on your LinkedIn profile. We will discuss that more specifically in future chapters.

TIP: Rarely does anyone use all the LinkedIn sections. Your profile will include only the right sections for you!

Demonstrate Your Expertise

Take *real action* to grow your personal brand in real life. Then share it on LinkedIn.

Action	Brand elements	LinkedIn sections
Speak	Thought leader	Video Portfolio, Experience
Teach	Thought leader	Experience, Summary
Research	Thought leader, learner	Summary, Experience
Mentor	Values	Summary
Advocate	Values, goals	Summary
Blog, write	Thought leader, values, goals, personality, story	LinkedIn Publisher, Publications
Share content	Thought leader	Status updates
Connect, join	Network, community	Connections, Organizations, Groups, Invitations, Messaging
Volunteer	Thought leader, sales, community	Volunteering, Summary, Publisher, Interests

Your personal brand is more than just where you work or study; it's more than the jobs you have had or the classes you've taken. It's an intangible asset and your strategic advantage. Your personal brand is a combination of many of your personal attributes, skills, and qualities. It's the intangible elements of your presence that make you unique. Your brand also incorporates your personality, values, vision, passions, goals, and strategic focus.

If you are a financial planner, engineer, salesperson, HR executive, or marketer, I doubt that you are identical to all the others in your field. This is true regarding your expertise as well as the most intangible aspects of your brand. Figure out how you can differentiate yourself from everyone else. It might be what you know or how you approach a problem. It might be your special personal qualities that make a difference.

TIP: If you are struggling to identify your brand elements, ask others for their feedback. Ask colleagues, clients, and even your kids!

Consider your professional goals as you think about your personal branding. Are you looking for a job, partner, new client, speaking engagement, or a specific business opportunity? Knowing this will help you be more specific and focused with the language on your profile.

Is your expertise general or specialized? It's much harder to be considered an expert of twenty things. Be selective and focus deeply on a couple of things. For example, a marketer may specialize in digital marketing for the insurance industry, a civil engineer may be an expert on a specific type of bridge construction, or a financial planner may serve specifically baby boomer women in transition.

Now take your brand a step further with your personal qualities. Here are some examples of how a personal brand might be described by others:

- financial advisor who is a strong listener and communicator and specializes in the baby boomer women's market
- executive recruiter in the energy industry who is helpful and persistent
- project manager specializing in document management with leadership and collaboration skills

---

What do people say about you? What do you want them to say about you? What are you doing about this?

Demonstrate, Don't Tell

Let's assume you are known as a great leader. I don't suggest stating on your LinkedIn profile that you are a great leader. Instead, demonstrate your leadership. Display your leadership roles and positions whether they are from professional or volunteer experience. Describe your leadership goals. Talk about your team. Demonstrate your leadership on LinkedIn.

Think about Lynn Garelick. She doesn't need to say she is a talented designer. She demonstrates her work and passions with images, projects, volunteering information, and organizational affiliations. She demonstrates her passion and interests, many of which tie into her design expertise.

It's Yours to Manage

You are in control of a large portion of the perspective that people have of you. You control your personal brand by the combination of your live actions and corresponding online profile. Your company expects this, although they may not be training you to do this. They should be!

Get Feedback

Ask others for feedback on your brand. Ask them about your best qualities and ways you may improve. Get real opinions on your personal and professional attributes. Do you know what people think of you? You need to be open to different perspectives. Don't be confined by job titles or past experiences.

Do you have gaps between what you have accomplished and where you see yourself? Take action! Volunteer for a special assignment at your company or school. Choose a project that lets you work on a specialized skill you are developing. Better yet, do this special project in conjunction with other people in a group setting. Volunteer for a difficult part of the mission. Your colleagues will notice.

Don't limit your thinking to your current workplace or classroom. Figure out: How do you add real organizational value? Where should I be volunteering or speaking to demonstrate my expertise and brand? What are your most significant accomplishments? What are you proud of professionally and personally?

"40% admit it's difficult to describe what they do for a living."

LinkedIn, May 26, 2016

Leverage LinkedIn for your personal branding. That's what this book is all about. The first part of this book is how to use your LinkedIn profile for your personal branding. The other opportunities we will cover include sharing content, making industry and community connections, and becoming a **thought leader** by blogging or sharing presentations.

Think first about your best authentic self as you prepare to write your entire LinkedIn profile. This evolving self-perception of your personal brand should guide you as you go through the profile writing process.

Let's now move to the next chapter where we will learn how to "be found" on LinkedIn.

LinkedIn Profile Sections

CHAPTER 3

Be Found and Contacted

This is a big reason we are here on LinkedIn. We want colleagues, clients, prospects, hiring managers, or candidates to find us online. Many experts will advise us about being found through LinkedIn search. My philosophy is that it is important to be found, but you want the viewer of your profile to relate to you and be interested in you once he or she arrives at your profile. So while being found is important, you want your profile to be interesting and compelling enough for a live follow-up, whether that is an interview, meeting, or conversation.

Make sure your profile leaves someone thinking, "I want to know more!" or "I have to meet this person as soon as possible!" or "We need that type of person on our team!"

Google and LinkedIn Searches

Most of us want to be found online when potential clients or prospects are looking for us by name or searching for specific capabilities. Many Google searches of individual names go straight to a LinkedIn profile. The Google search algorithm ranks the LinkedIn website very highly, so not having a profile is a huge disadvantage for today's professional. Some consultants and attorneys now open their practice with a LinkedIn profile before building a company website.

You can also be found through the LinkedIn search by name, company, geography, or even keywords related to your specialties. So it makes sense to use the words that are most appropriate for your business, practice, or career. Being specific is optimal. For an attorney, keywords such as divorce, family law, intellectual property, corporate law, or real estate might make sense in addition to the words attorney and lawyer.

Using the right words is not only a search strategy. You want to choose words that resonate with your client. Speaking the right "industry language" can make a difference in how comfortable your client is with you once you have been found. So I believe that the words you choose can be very powerful indeed!

LinkedIn's search function is important for everyone, but especially for those in a job search or those who are recruiters on the other side of the career table. Keywords are one of the ways that other LinkedIn users will find you. (These will be discussed in-depth in the next chapter.) In addition to keywords, the activity that you have will impact your ability to be found.

Think about this search power. LinkedIn has very high Search Engine Optimization (SEO) ranking authority with Google. Once your profile is optimized, you can expect your LinkedIn profile to rank higher than most of the other content displayed on Google. You want your LinkedIn profile to become the main focal point for any online search. If your name is associated with negative online articles or comments, those posts usually appear lower on a Google search page once your profile is complete and optimized.

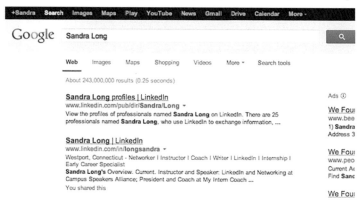

Focus on the Positive and Professional Online

For example, LinkedIn profiles typically **appear first** in a Google name search. If you have any negative search results, expect them to be moved to a lower position on the page once your LinkedIn profile is complete and optimized.

This might include the following:

- arrest reports
- negative press
- lawsuits or legal reports
- old or out-of-date professional information

Take the time now to also clean up any negative Facebook, Twitter, Instagram, or YouTube activity. Remove posts that will embarrass you later.

Fortunately, you can count on your LinkedIn profile to rise high in Google ranking and represent your best professional self. Having a "complete" profile is the major starting point to accomplish "being found" online.

---

100 Percent Complete Profile

LinkedIn has a "completeness barometer." This minimum threshold will determine your fate for LinkedIn search success. As of this writing, the exact completeness requirement listed on LinkedIn includes the following:

- your industry and location
- an up-to-date current position (with a description)
- two past positions
- your education
- your skills (minimum of three)
- a profile photo
- at least fifty connections

Before We Begin Making Changes

Decide if you want to announce profile changes to your network. If you wish to temporarily "shut off" this notification, first go to Privacy and Settings, which you will find at the upper right-hand corner of your profile. Under the Privacy tab, select "Sharing profile edits" as shown below:

Click "Sharing profile edits" and set to "no" and save.

Your Name Matters

Your name on LinkedIn will obviously help people find you! One of the most common ways for your colleagues and associates to search for you will be typing your name into either Google or LinkedIn. Most Google searches for names lead to a LinkedIn profile. If your name is common, the search result will show all the people with your exact name.

There are some important factors about your name to consider. Use the name field properly to avoid LinkedIn account problems and confusion. Be aware that LinkedIn is very strict about the name field.

Display only your real name on LinkedIn. Don't use the LinkedIn personal profile for a company, organization, or group. The personal profile page is designed for a real person only. Do not put contact information in the name field, as this is strictly prohibited by the LinkedIn user agreement.

Make sure your full name is spelled properly and consistently across your other social media, résumé, bios, and websites. The first letter of your first and last name should be capitalized. All other letters should be lower case. Occasionally, I see a name in all lower or uppercase letters, and it looks unprofessional. Using all uppercase letters online is synonymous with shouting.

You may wish to show a maiden or former name in the name field. If LinkedIn users may be looking for you using your former name, then by all means, show it. Edit the name field and add the former name under the Former Name section. This is an example of the LinkedIn display:

Jane (Smith) Jones

You are currently permitted to add your certifications or suffixes in the name field after your last name. Use this if you believe your certifications are specifically being used in a search. Simply add the certification after the last name field.

Examples:
Jane Jones PhD
James Smith MSW
Felix Giannini FPE, CPP

Also, make sure you add the details of your special designations in the Certifications section as described in chapter 8.

Some of us have name variations or alternative spellings. If you have common misspellings or variations, add this information to the bottom of your Summary (or Advice for Contacting) section but not in the official name field. To do this, indicate "common misspellings" and then list them specifically.

Industry and Location

At the top of your profile, you have an opportunity to declare your location and industry. Take the time to make the right choices. For the industry designation, you will need to select from the choices provided from the drop-down menu that LinkedIn provides. If you can't find an exact match in the menu, select the one that's the closest to your function or industry.

For location, there are a couple of options. I am personally suspicious when I see a profile location listed as a specific country such as France, United States, Australia, or Canada. I would rather see a city or regional area listed as a location. Normally, by entering your postal or city code, most of us choose either the local town or the greater metropolitan area.

For example, I can choose "Westport, Connecticut," or "Greater New York City Area." Depending on your personal brand and LinkedIn goals, you can select what makes the most sense for you. Since my customers are global, I select "Greater New York City Area."

If you are a local shopkeeper in "Bellevue, Washington," however, you might decide to choose "Bellevue" over "Greater Seattle Area." If you are a job seeker or sales professional covering the state, select "Greater Seattle Area." Many of us will choose the large metropolitan area if we are looking for clients in the larger geography.

Here is a screenshot example:

Greater New York City Area | Professional Training & Coaching

"More than 30% of recruiters use location when searching for candidates, so make sure you add your location, making it easier for them to find you."

LinkedIn, May 26, 2016

Custom URL

LinkedIn gives users an opportunity for a customized URL corresponding to your individual profile. I recommend choosing a URL that is as close to your name as possible. You will have your own URL for the profile page, which is more attractive if you customize it.

Example of a URL likely to be assigned by LinkedIn:
www.linkedin.com/in/felix-giannini-c765aa2

Example of a customized URL:
www.linkedin.com/in/felixgiannini

Why customize this? Because it gives you the opportunity

- to have a more attractive professional link;
- to use it on your e-mail signature, résumé, website, and business cards; and
- to improve search hits.

What's the best way to customize the URL? I recommend you try to get your exact first and last name. Keep in mind there are no spaces or capital letters. Don't select a company name for your URL.

If your name is more common, it is likely that your first choice for the vanity URL will not be available. Consider adding a middle initial. Also, LinkedIn will recommend alternative versions for you to consider. For many of us with common names, you will have to choose the best alternative. Whatever you choose is likely to be far better than the URL assigned automatically by LinkedIn.

Public Profile

Make your LinkedIn profile visible on Google search. Simply make sure your public profile is properly set up as "Visible to everyone." You can do this while editing your personal URL. You may want to double check these settings to be sure you are visible. Select each box for the profile elements. See below:

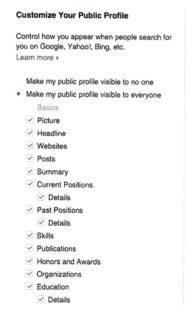

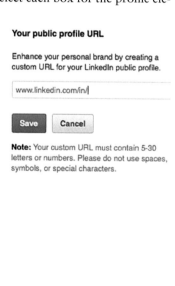

Contact Information

In addition to being found through the search engines, I am a big believer in the importance of liberally sharing contact information on your profile. What's the point of being found when your prospect can't call or e-mail you? I see this mistake every day on LinkedIn profiles!

All LinkedIn users need to be sure to completely fill out the Contact Info section and the Advice for Contacting section. In the Contact Info section, add your personal or company website, Twitter handle, phone number, e-mail, and work address.

Example from Contact Info Section

Email	sandra@postroadconsulting.com	Phone	203-221-2649 (work)
		Address	191 Post Road West Westport CT 06880
Twitter	SandraGLong		
Websites	Sandra Long on SlideShare Post Road Consulting Facebook Post Road Consulting Website		

Advice for Contacting is one of the optional add-on sections you don't want to miss. Give your viewers the best advice to contact you. If you prefer e-mail or texting, this is a perfect place to set expectations about your availability and response time. I like to have a friendly message that invites new contacts and introductions. You may also want to add in your other web or social media addresses for additional contact and engagement.

Your prospects may want to call or e-mail you directly after viewing your profile, so make it easy for them to find this information. I also suggest adding your contact information at the bottom of your Summary if possible. (I will remind you of this again in chapter 9 when we discuss summaries.) Letting people know how to contact or follow you is a top priority!

Company Page

In addition to your personal LinkedIn profile, you may want to consider a company page if you are an owner of a company or the marketing leader. There is a direct correlation between the personal brand of employees and a company brand. The company brand should be reflected in the employee profiles, just as the personal employee profiles impact their employer's brand. Read more about company pages in chapter 12.

Who's Viewed Your Profile?

"Who's Viewed Your Profile" is an extremely popular feature on LinkedIn. Increasing the number of profile views is a top online networking goal for most people. I usually kick off my LinkedIn networking workshop discussing this very point. Of course, you will be more motivated to increase views if you are very comfortable with your LinkedIn profile and brand.

We know that the "100 percent complete" benchmark mentioned above is critical to LinkedIn SEO and your ability to be found through advanced search. According to LinkedIn, you are far more likely to have your profile viewed if you are showing a photo and your skills. You will also likely be viewed more often if you have a large number of connections.

LinkedIn SEO is a hot topic. People want to know how to increase profile views with an optimized profile. I think this is extremely important, especially for active job seekers. However, my philosophy is that personal branding and activity is more powerful than hardcore SEO tactics for most professionals.

Your offline and online activity will dramatically impact the number of views to your profile. If you are actively involved in business or community, your views will reflect that activity. So if you are going on sales calls, meeting with partners, interviewing, speaking, teaching, writing, or meeting people, you can count on more LinkedIn profile views.

Additionally, your online activity has a direct correlation to profile views. If you are adding connections, posting articles, making mentions, recommending, endorsing, or liking posts, you are more likely to be seen and then your profile viewed. If you are viewing other people's profiles, they are likely to come back and look at yours. If you are involved in several groups, making comments, and sharing, your visibility will rise.

Ways That Your Activities Increase Views to Your Profile

Online activity to increase views to your profile	Offline activity to increase views to your profile
Looking at other LinkedIn profiles	Speaking
InMail messaging or connecting	Making sales calls
Liking or commenting on content	Attending meetings or events
Publishing LinkedIn blog articles	Teaching or mentoring
LinkedIn status updates or mentions	Conducting interviews
Sending LinkedIn invitations	Calling or e-mailing someone
Participating in LinkedIn Groups	Participating in organizations
Blogging on any website	Writing a book or paper
Recommendations and endorsements	Getting referred or making referral
All other social media activity	Making an introduction

Your activity, both offline and online, will impact your number of profile views on LinkedIn. Make sure you understand the etiquette around all your online actions. Gain a clear view and understanding of what is private messaging versus public posting of content. I also want to caution not to overdo your activity, because you don't want to turn off your network from overexposure. Your connections have the option to either unconnect with you or unfollow your posts if your posts are annoying them in any way.

LinkedIn Fun Fact: LinkedIn is serving more than two hundred countries and territories.

LinkedIn

Now that we have a sense of how to be found on LinkedIn, it is time to dive a bit deeper to learn more about keywords and language in chapter 4.

Resources for Chapter 3

Register at the companion website (http://www.linkedinforpersonalbranding .com) for information on the following:

- names allowed on LinkedIn
- how to change how your name appears on the profile
- Former Name, Maiden Name, or Nickname on LinkedIn
- how to add certifications to your name on LinkedIn
- LinkedIn's definition of a 100 percent complete profile
- how to change the company or industry on your profile
- how to change the location on your profile
- how to add or edit contact information
- how to customize public profile URL
- LinkedIn public profile

CHAPTER 4

Selecting the Right Words and Language

The language and wording you select may have a bearing on who finds you and will definitely create an impression once they are reading your profile. Language and specific word choices impact your personal brand.

Select the right industry language in an interview, in a sales meeting, or on a profile to distinguish yourself from an outsider. In deciding about your word choice, think about your entire audience and most especially your targeted prospect. If you are too much of an industry language geek, will that be a benefit or a deterrent for you? If you are a college student breaking into a new industry, your knowledge of industry terms and concepts, used appropriately, can make you stand out from the crowd.

Is First Person Right for You?

One major language decision is whether you write your profile in the first, second, or third person. I always recommend writing in first person to make the profile more compelling and story-like. Here are the options below.

Person	Examples of words	
First	I, me, mine, my, we, us, our, ours	Written from a writer's point of view. Used for memoirs, letters, stories, autobiographies, and social profiles.
Second	You, your, yours	Directed to the reader. Used for letters, advertisements, and occasionally for profiles.
Third	He, she, it, him, her, Mr. Smith, Ms. Jones	Outside narrators view. Used for academic articles, traditional biographies, and profiles.

I recommend that you keep your profile consistent with first person throughout your profile. If you decide on third person, keep that consistent too (across summary and all other profile sections). In my experience, a great majority of LinkedIn experts recommend using first person for a profile, but some users will insist on third person. The individual user needs to be comfortable with his or her own profile, so I always keep that in mind.

Keywords

Keywords are a hot topic because the LinkedIn platform has extensive search capabilities. Not only can everyone search by keyword through the LinkedIn's Advanced Search function, but many companies use the premium Recruiter service to search for talent. Using the LinkedIn Recruiter service, human resources and talent professionals search by keywords, experience, skills, geography, and other fields to create a targeted candidate list.

As you consider your keywords, be aware that there are many variations of phrases and words. Searching on Google is not always the same as on LinkedIn. Translate your keywords to the role being searched for and think about all the possibilities.

You need help with	Possible Google search	Possible LinkedIn search and keywords
Taxes	"Help with taxes or accounting" or "How to reduce my tax bill"	Accountant or CPA or certified public accountant
Growing your business	"How to grow my business" or "How to increase sales"	Business coach or marketing consultant or marketing expert or sales coach or sales trainer
Problem landlord	"Sue my landlord" or "Find a new apartment"	Attorney or lawyer or realtor
Helping child get into the right college	"Best colleges" or "How to evaluate or find the best college"	College consultant or educational counselor or college admissions expert

Keywords should be an accurate reflection of you, your experience, and your brand. Consider what you want to be found for and what you want to be hired for. There are so many variations of words in the English language. For example, web, digital, and online marketing. Which wording do you choose? And how else can you find the right keywords?

Keyword Research

Keywords and choice of language is important for everyone, not just job seekers. Do your own brainstorming and consider asking friends. In addition, here are ten potential ways to research for the most impactful keywords and language:

1. **Look at five to ten of your ideal companies or prospects.** Read about them in general and also check out their career pages for clues to the language and wording that they are using.

2. **Take a look at several job descriptions of positions you would love.** Find the words they are regularly using and see if you can incorporate them into your profile naturally. Or consider putting the description into a word cloud to determine what words are being used most prevalently.

3. **Look at people on LinkedIn who have the job you want.** What words and language are they using? Do those words apply to you? If yes, use them naturally. Check out your competitors and industry colleagues.

4. **Use the LinkedIn skills section by considering the drop-down suggestions offered by LinkedIn as you add a new skill.** Or dig deeper behind skills to identify other users or presentations that may offer better clues.

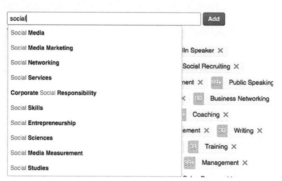

5. **Look at free online keyword tools from Google to see which of your industry words are being searched more commonly online.**

6. **Study the wording used on job board listings.** Check out Indeed, Monster, and SimplyHired since they are all very popular boards. Or look at a niche job board if appropriate to your goals.

7. **Look at the profiles of LinkedIn influencers that you follow in your industry.** Check out the skills that they display or write about in a blog post. Pick those that are most strategic to you.

8. **Check out your LinkedIn Groups to find industry appropriate language and keywords.**

9. **Look in the LinkedIn Jobs tab for keyword clues.** You will find job descriptions embedded within LinkedIn.

10. **Do a little digging in your University Alumni Finder page on LinkedIn.** Select your desired job and city. LinkedIn will offer the "What they are skilled at" list, which you can draw from.

Consider using your keywords throughout your LinkedIn profile, but make sure the wording sounds natural and is an accurate portrayal of your capabilities. The keywords are especially powerful when located in your headline and job titles. Other good sections in which to use keywords are the Summary, Skills, Experience, Description, and Interests sections.

LinkedIn Fun Fact: The most overused word on LinkedIn profiles is "motivated."

LinkedIn, 2016

One thing I want to caution is not to overload or "stuff" the keywords. Don't have profile sections where you are just listing keywords over and over again. I do like a specialties list at the end of a summary, but that should do it for listing keywords. It's far better to have an authentic, natural, friendly, helpful-sounding profile than to have a lot of words jammed into your profile.

Action Verbs and Metrics

Use strong action verbs and metrics on your profile, especially in the Experience section. This is the same advice you will hear from a résumé expert. Instead of saying, "Responsible for sales and marketing," consider stating this with stronger language and specific statistics. "Increased sales by 12 percent over the prior year" would be a stronger alternative. Transform any weak language to verbs, achievements, and accomplishments.

Examples of Strong Action Verbs

Past Tense for Previous Experience Profile Section

Built, sold, presented, created, launched, wrote, developed, initiated

Present Tense for Current Experience Profile Section

Building, selling, presenting, creating, launching, writing, developing, initiating

---

Language Is Power

Be authentic, accurate, and truthful at all times. Use the powerful tool of language to differentiate yourself and be found. Now we will move on to chapter 5 and discover how to make your brand more visual.

Resources for Chapter 4

Register at the companion website (http://www.linkedinforpersonalbranding .com) for information on the following:

- LinkedIn Jobs tab—to help with keyword research and job search
- LinkedIn alumni tool—to help with keyword research and networking
- action verbs (download)

CHAPTER 5

Your Visual Brand

Images, Rich Media, and Links

LinkedIn has become increasingly visual. Use this to your advantage to enhance your personal brand. Now you can add some visual energy to your profile page with rich media and links.

Headshot

Let's start with your headshot, which is an essential part of your profile. Your prospects and clients want to find, retain, refer, or hire someone who demonstrates success and a strong personal brand. Therefore, a headshot is a necessity. Make sure you are smiling and professionally attired. If you can afford a professional photographer, it is usually the best investment you can make in your personal brand and self-confidence.

If your company has a website with biography pages, you can use your new headshot in both places. Ask the photographer to create two versions including one that is optimally sized for uploading into LinkedIn. Ask your marketing team to link the website biography page over to your LinkedIn profile, which will have more detail than the company web page of biographies.

Pick the Right Headshot for Your Profile

This photo is not suitable for a LinkedIn headshot.

Generally you want a headshot photo that does not look like a "body shot." You want a photo that emphasizes your face and smile (above the shoulders) not your waist or body.

This photo may be fine for Facebook.

This is not a headshot. This photo is perfect for Facebook.

The headshot photo on the left is perfect. The headshot on the right is too small and blurry for use on LinkedIn.

TIP: Get a headshot that you love. You will feel more confident.

LinkedIn Fun Fact: Your profile is twenty-one times more likely to be viewed and you are thirty-six times more likely to receive a LinkedIn message if you have a photo on your LinkedIn profile.

LinkedIn, August 3, 2016

Background Image

LinkedIn introduced the background banner feature for personal profiles in 2014. This is a great upgrade for your visual brand. Many long time LinkedIn users are not taking advantage of this exciting feature.

Your background banner should match your personal and professional brand. The banner helps reinforce your unique value from a career or sales perspective. There are many options that work well, including the following.

Company- or Team-Branded Banner for Employees

This type of banner is suitable for an entire company, a department, or a small team.

- custom banner to match your website and logo
- image of product or service provided by your company
- image of your workplace
- image of customers using the company's product or service
- custom banner for your department, team, or brand
- image of the entire team working together or posing

Personal Professional Banners

This type of banner is perfect for consultants, job seekers, entrepreneurs, and company employees.

- image of you in a professional setting
- image of you speaking or leading your team
- image as you are presented with an award
- image of your product or service
- word cloud about you
- image from your industry
- image montage of your customers or products

Geographic Banners

This type of banner is suitable for anyone but is particularly powerful for realtors and geographically oriented business professionals.

- city skyline
- harbor view of your city
- map of your region
- image of your town square
- image of a city landmark

Call-to-Action Banners

Sales teams may want to display a banner with a "call to action" message such as an offer for an audit, meeting, or phone call.

Examples of Effective Background Banners or "Hero Images"

Example 1: Felix Giannini, CEO of Lexco Inc., displays his typical customer sites.

Example 2: Mark Ehrenzeller displays the Boston skyline. Mark is president of Frank I. Rounds Company in Randolph, Massachusetts. They service the Greater Boston area.

Images

Your banner images should be sized properly (see appendix). Note that the display area for the LinkedIn banner is extremely limited because your headshot and LinkedIn ads can obscure some of the lower part of the banner.

Be sure to display images with proper permission. Don't just grab an image from a website or Google. Here are several good options:

- photos you have taken yourself (high resolution)
- images you have personally designed
- images that you own or have purchased
- free images from online sites

For "free" images, look for those that are clearly labeled as "available for commercial use" and are "attribution free." This means that you can use them however you wish, but never claim them as your own.

Your LinkedIn background banner should match your personal and company brand. Be consistent between all the words and images on your profile for the best effect. The banner is a big component of your brand.

Professional Portfolio: Add Rich Media to Your Profile

The rich media opportunities from the professional portfolio sections on LinkedIn bring your personal brand to the next level. This is often the best way to demonstrate your skills and accomplishments.

Consider adding slide presentations, images, or videos to your LinkedIn profile under the Experience, Education, or Summary sections. My favorites are SlideShare and YouTube, which I display on my profile.

Pick the videos and presentations that are the best match for your brand. Make sure the videos are professional in nature and relevant to your brand and profession. You may upload images or videos or add a link for YouTube or SlideShare.

Your professional portfolio of rich media links can be added to your Summary, Experience, or Education sections.

Author Example

My professional portfolio on LinkedIn is always changing. I use photos, SlideShare presentations, and YouTube videos under my Experience and Summary sections. My portfolio examples are as follows:

@ Cornell University - Ithaca New York   Click thru to learn more about training

Connecticut Bar Associatio...   Boston Social Selling Work...   With Entrepreneur Audience

˅ SEE MORE ˅

Other Important Links

In the Contact Us section at the top of your profile, be sure to include your Twitter handle, your website links, and your social media links in addition to your regular contact information. You can also add a link to your social media profile pages under Experience or Summary if you prefer.

Don't Forget eBay, Amazon, and Wikipedia

Many of my clients have connected their various online stores and profiles with their LinkedIn profile. One of my retail clients had employees add their eBay store link to employee profiles during LinkedIn training. If you are an author, you can link your Amazon author page or the book link with your LinkedIn profile. (See chapter 8 for two author examples using the LinkedIn Profile Publications section.) If you have a page on Wikipedia, you can link from LinkedIn to your Wikipedia page.

The images, links, and rich media that you select for your LinkedIn profile should be just as strategic as the words and language. Have fun and use the professional portfolio sections to your advantage.

Now that we have covered language, images, and links, it's time to dive into actual profile sections. The best place to start is with your experience. Join me in the next chapter called "Your Experience Brand."

Resources for Chapter 5

Chapter 17: Thought Leader: SlideShare and Video
Appendix C, for image specifications

Register at the companion website (http://www.linkedinforpersonalbranding .com) for information on the following:

- how to add or edit work samples (also called professional portfolio or rich media)
- how to add or edit your profile photo or headshot
- profile photo (headshot) guidelines
- how to add or change background photo (banner)
- LinkedIn background banner ideas (SlideShare)

CHAPTER 6

Your Professional Experience Brand

Your work experience is a critical section of your LinkedIn profile because it is typically the best example of your professional accomplishments. Make it compelling by writing in the first person. It is also a great place to use industry language, keywords, action verbs, links, and images to complement and enhance your brand.

A June 2016 survey conducted by Post Road Consulting LLC found that more than 70 percent of LinkedIn users felt that the Summary and Experience sections were the most important sections to express their personal brand effectively on LinkedIn.

For each position that you list in the Experience section, include the title, company name, location, dates, and description. When you add a company name, select it from the drop-down menu, if available, so that you can display the company logo on your profile page. This logo is also a link to your employer's company page. As an employee, your personal profile is also an extension of your employer's brand.

Accuracy matters. Make sure that the dates in your Experience sections match your résumé dates exactly. Recruiters often eliminate potential candidates displaying inconsistent dates (LinkedIn profile vs. résumé). However, don't make the mistake of just copying your résumé language word for word. Make sure the Experience section is strategic and focuses on your best achievements. Use strong action verbs wherever possible. Add keywords authentically. Focus on outcomes over responsibilities.

TIP: A LinkedIn profile should not be the same as a résumé!

Consider confidentiality when writing about your experience on your profile. Many times on profiles I will see accomplishments and become concerned about confidentiality. Be certain that the information you're sharing on LinkedIn is information that can be shared online. For example, company financial or legal information that may be appropriate for a résumé should not always be shared online.

TIP: Pull out any confidential information.

The LinkedIn Work Experience section is especially powerful because of these special attributes:

- **Section links.** You can link many other profile sections to work experience for greater emphasis. These include organizations, projects, and awards. (See chapter 8.)
- **Work examples or "professional portfolio."** For each Experience section, you have the opportunity to upload work samples such as videos, images, or presentations. (See chapter 5 about the professional portfolio.)
- **Recommendations.** Written testimonials from your clients and coworkers are connected to your experience (or education). Try to get recommendations that are associated with each of your positions. (See chapter 10.)
- **Position title.** This is a great opportunity to use more relevant keywords and not just the exact position title.
- **Company logos and links.** If your employer has a company page, your profile may have a company logo and direct link to the page.

Let's dive deeper into the Experience section to make sure you are optimizing this critical area. Not only is this a keyword-rich part of your profile, but it also contains the "meat" that your prospects may be looking for.

List multiple positions. In most cases, it is wise to list all your jobs, titles, locations, and descriptions of these in your LinkedIn profile. People may decide to connect with you if they are reminded that you were once coworkers by seeing your early experiences on your profile. LinkedIn recommends showing your current role and the past two positions, at a minimum.

Doing more than one job? List them all on your profile. More and more people are working a day job and also moonlighting as a blogger, speaker, consultant, or small business owner. For most corporate employees, it makes sense to discuss your activities with your boss before adding to your profile. Most likely, it's an important conversation for you to have anyway. Your Summary will be the key in how you spin all of this together successfully. (Learn about the weaver persona in chapter 9.)

Do you have a gap in employment? Above all, make sure your employment dates are accurate. Don't be tempted to adjust your dates because that is an immediate red flag for a recruiter. Consider beefing up your other accomplishments, such as volunteering, during employment gaps.

Combining work experience at one company might make sense. If you have had multiple positions within one company over many years, it might be wise to combine them into a grouping. You would need to consider that they should be similar types of positions and that they can be easily described within the description.

> Example: Let's assume that you had three different sales positions with a company over a span of five years. You might logically combine the three roles into one Experience section on LinkedIn. Within the description, you can then segment each position specifically with specific titles, dates, and accomplishments.

If you are a job seeker, be more careful about combining positions. It is best to show your most recent position as between two and five years because recruiters may sort potential candidates based on a "time in position" factor. I suspect if you are showing the same position for ten years, you may be putting yourself out of contention. Of course, you want to honestly show your experience. I am simply suggesting that you may choose not to combine your current position for that reason.

One very common mistake is leaving the description blank. Don't miss this valuable opportunity. Common wisdom dictates that you focus more heavily on your accomplishments rather than your responsibilities. However, there are several effective ways to leverage the description portion. Some examples may include the following.

Types of Experience Sections

Accomplishment: This is a very popular format for the Work Experience description. You may start off with a short description of the work being performed with each experience, followed by a list of résumé-like accomplishments using action verbs and keywords. This is the usually the best format for both active and passive job seekers.

Role and company: Describe the role you have within the company in the first paragraph. Add a brief company description in the second paragraph. This can be an effective format for an employee or company leader but is not usually recommended for a job seeker. Job seekers who use this format should consider adding in their specific accomplishments and leverage appropriate keywords and action verbs.

Role definition: If you are acting in several unique capacities, consider describing your various roles.

Client types: Describe your top client types and the typical work you do. You may list them as functional client types (HR, marketing, engineering) or more broadly (nonprofit, university, corporate).

Approach: Describe your overall work and then add your unique work process or approach.

Consider combining these approaches if that makes more sense for you. You have quite a bit of flexibility as you describe your work experience. I do want to caution you to be aware of how you are using your LinkedIn summary (chapter 9) and keeping the two distinct and complementary of each other.

TIP: The Work Experience section is strictly about your work at company X, while your summary is more strategic and typically about you in general.

Example 1: Accomplishment

Notice the strong use of action verbs such as launched, improved, increased, and implemented. (Past tense is used for previous experience.)

Vice President Operations

DEQ LLC

January 2006 – January 2010 (4 years 1 month) | Greater New York City Area

Directed overall operations of a SAAS company, with accountability for strategic planning, P & L, sales & marketing, and customer service. Existing customer base of 3500 active global users.

• Launched three new SAAS solutions and increased sales by 27% in 2008.
• Improved first call close ratio by an average of 15% YOY between 2006 - 2008.
• Increased customer satisfaction and decreased call volume from new customers as a result of implementing a new call center support system.
• Implemented employee reward system and reduced employee turnover by 8% in 2007 and 9% in 2008.

Example 2: Merged Experience

When merging two positions into one Experience section, it usually makes sense to list the current and most senior-level position as the title for the combined section. The other option is to list both titles.

Before

Senior Sales Representative
EENG Inc
January 2013 – September 2013 (9 months) I Greater Chicago Area

Sold EENG products for an expanded Chicago territory and three major accounts. Achieved or exceeded all monthly sales goals while in this position.

Sales Representative
EENG Inc
January 2012 – January 2013 (1 year 1 month) I Greater Chicago Area

Sold EENG products in a geographic territory outside of Chicago. Exceeded sales quota by 13% in first year.

After

Senior Sales Representative
EENG Inc
January 2012 – September 2013 (1 year 9 months) I Greater Chicago Area

I had two Sales positions with increasing responsibility:

Senior Sales Representative: From January 2013 - September 2013
Sold EENG products for an expanded Chicago territory and three major accounts. Achieved or exceeded all monthly sales goals while in this position.

Sales Representative: From January 2012 - January 2013
Sold EENG products in a geographic territory outside of Chicago. Exceeded sales quota by 13% in first year.

Example 3: "Define Your Roles"

This is written in the present tense (current position). The four critical action verbs are highlighted in this example (coaching, training, speaking, and blogging).

 Experience

Vice President, Coach, Speaker, Trainer, Blogger
Gilbert Consulting Partners
January 2013 – Present (3 years 5 months) I Santa Fe, New Mexico Area

I am one of three partners at Gilbert Consulting Partners. We specialize in global leadership development programs. My personal expertise and contribution to the business are in the categories of coaching, corporate training, speaking, and blogging.

COACHING
* One on one executive leadership coaching
* Team coaching

CORPORATE TRAINING
* Workshop facilitator
* Program design

SPEAKING
* Corporate events for employees
* HR Conferences

BLOGGING
* Company website
* LinkedIn platform
* Guest blogging on several major HR sites

Example 4: Client Types

 Experience

Vice President, Coach, Speaker, Trainer, Blogger
Gilbert Consulting Partners
January 2013 – Present (3 years 5 months) | Santa Fe, New Mexico Area

I am one of three partners at Gilbert Consulting Partners. We specialize in global leadership development programs. My personal expertise and contribution to the business are in the categories of coaching, corporate training, speaking, and blogging. We revolve our custom programs around our specific customers. Our customers and programs include:

CORPORATE
Large Enterprise Companies - Team Workshops
Small Medium Businesses - Team Workshop and CEO Roundtable

NON-PROFIT
Executive Director Leadership Academy

GOVERNMENT
Washington DC Annual Leadership Summit

Example 5: Role and Company

The Experience section for Craig Flaherty, of Redniss & Mead, is shown below. Craig describes his role and his company. Craig also includes four organizations and a video (professional portfolio) that demonstrates the work of his firm. Notice the logo of Redniss & Mead in his Experience section.

Senior Engineer and Principal   REDNISS
Redniss & Mead, Inc.   & MEAD
January 2006 – Present (10 years 1 month) | Stamford, CT

I am a principal with the firm heading larger and more complex civil engineering design and land use permitting projects. As Senior Engineer, I oversee the work of Project Engineers providing guidance, quality control, and mentoring. I am also responsible for guiding company IT systems and support and company branding and marketing.

Redniss & Mead, Inc. is a consulting and design firm specializing in Site Civil Engineering, Land Surveying, Planning & Zoning Consulting, and Permitting. Located in Stamford, CT, the company has established itself as a leading land-use consultant in the region, providing services from project inception to the design and permit phase and through completion of construction.

▾ 4 organizations

American Society of Civil Engineers   **Sewer Commission, Darien**
View↓   View↓

Environmental Protection Commission,   **Building Board of Appeals, Darien**
Darien   View↓
View↓

Convent of the Sacred Heart

Who Are You?

If you're just starting out . . .	Include your internships
If you've held many positions at the same company . . .	Consider consolidating
If you're a job seeker . . .	Focus on specific accomplishments, action verbs, and keywords within the description
If you're a company recruiter . . .	Consider describing the company culture and why employees love to work at your company
If you're a consultant . . .	Consider describing your customers or processes
If you're starting over in a new industry . . .	Be sure to describe transferrable skills and use the summary as a bridge to new opportunities

Keep Your Positions Up to Date

Do your best to keep your positions up to date in the Experience section of your profile. This can be tricky if you have recently separated from a company role. One way to handle this is to create a new experience such as the following:

> "Marketing executive open to field marketing positions" (LinkedIn, August 3, 2016)
> or
> Finance executive open to CFO or controller positions

LinkedIn Fun Fact: If your positions are kept up to date, your profile is eighteen times more likely to be found.

LinkedIn August 3, 2016

Final Tips

Finally, watch the little details like spelling, grammar, and punctuation. Make sure your previous positions are written in the past tense. Your current experience should be written in present tense.

Stay away from "responsible for this" and "responsible for that"—instead use action-oriented verbs and language that is more powerful. I also prefer using the first person in this section to make it more interesting and personal.

Now we are ready to move on to education and learning, an increasingly powerful element of your personal brand.

Resources for Chapter 6

Chapter 4: Selecting the Right Words and Language
Appendix C, for character count specifications

Register at the companion website (http://www.linkedinforpersonalbranding .com) for information on the following:

- action verbs (download)
- how to edit the Experience section
- how to add a company logo (associate employee with a company)

CHAPTER 7

Your Education and Learning Brand

Your "learning brand" is increasingly important. The world is changing so fast that learning ability and motivation is a key indicator of success. What you have learned, how you learn, and your continuous learning are part of what I like to call your "learning brand."

Your education and learning is reflected throughout your LinkedIn profile. The "learning"-related sections included in this chapter are as follows:

> Education
> Courses
> Certifications
> Test Scores and Awards

Let's start at the top with Education.

Education Section

The Education section is so important to LinkedIn that it's a required element of a complete profile. Be sure to list the school exactly and use the drop-down list so that you can display the university logo. Don't forget to add the exact degree and major for each college. There is also space to provide a bit of information about your activities.

Colgate University
Bachelor of Arts (B.A.), History
2004 – 2008

Activities and Societies: Phi Kappa Tau

Multiple Colleges and Universities

I recommend you show all the higher education institutions that you attended. There may be special exceptions, but this is the general rule or best practice. LinkedIn also allows you to rearrange the order of your schools very easily. If you never attended university or college, make absolutely sure you enter your high school in the Education section so that your profile is considered 100 percent complete.

High School

Many people include their high school or prep school as well. The decision to enter your high school is certainly optional. However, if you never attended college, you should definitely include your high school information. LinkedIn considers a profile complete only if the Education section has an entry. Many of us have significant friendships and connections from high school, so it is often a good idea to include this for networking reasons.

LOCAL TIP: Consider also including your high school if it is local where you do business. This shows your local roots, which is often very desirable. Residential real estate is a perfect example of a situation where you would definitely show your local high school if you are now selling in your hometown.

Courses

List courses in the Courses section of the LinkedIn profile. This is an especially powerful way to highlight the recent or strategic courses you have taken for your industry or career. It is not necessary to list all of your college courses, but consider adding those that are unique or related to your current or future work. If you are working your way through a career transition, the courses you display can be very impactful.

Certifications

I recommend documenting all certifications and licenses under the Certifications section. You occasionally see people put their professional designations under Education, and I recommend reserving that section for higher education and high school. Use the Certification section for your designations, certifications, and licenses.

Certifications are extremely important for certain industries and professions. In the finance industry, the Series 7, Series 63, and many other FINRA designations are absolutely essential for qualification at many financial positions. There are also certifications for project managers, engineers, real estate professionals, and so on.

Examples of Professional Designations

Profession	Certification	Full name
Accounting	CPA	Certified public accountant
Financial	CFA	Chartered financial advisor
Financial	CFP	Certified financial planner
Operations	PMP	Project management professional
Engineering	CCIE	Cisco certified internetwork expert
Human resources	PHR	Professional human resources
Coach	MCC	Master certified coach

Under the Certifications section in LinkedIn, you will be listing the name of the certification, the certifying authority, license number, the certification URL and the applicable dates. In some cases, the license number is not necessary for your profile, but the name and certifying authority are essential.

The authority is the organization that provides the certification such as FINRA, PMI, Microsoft, or your state.

Prioritize your certifications. Rearrange the order of your certifications so your most strategic ones are on top. At some point, you may choose to delete old and irrelevant certifications.

Pick the certifications that fit your personal brand and delete the remainder. I just removed a certification for Six Sigma Quality (Yellow Belt) that I received while working at Pitney Bowes. Even though I was proud of it, that particular certification does not fit with my brand and current role.

Example 1: Financial Professional Certifications with FINRA Logo

Certifications

Series 3
Financial Industry Regulatory Authority (FINRA)

FINra

Series 7
Financial Industry Regulatory Authority (FINRA)

FINra

Example 2: Microsoft Certification with Logo

Microsoft Certified Solutions Developer (MCSD)
Microsoft
2000 – 2001

Test Scores and GPA

I am generally not a fan of adding test scores or a GPA to a LinkedIn profile. This is especially true of a mature worker who has been out of college for several years. Your SAT, GRE, or GMAT score is just too much information in my opinion. Even your score for the tough Series 7 seems like overkill.

You will have to make your own decision about this based on your job status and industry. Some new graduates in certain industries may feel that test scores or GPA will be an advantage, but I believe that is more appropriate for a résumé. This is my personal opinion, and I suspect others may disagree. If you have a high GPA and high test scores, you will likely have academic honors that are a different story in my book.

Academic Honors

I love to see academic honors on a LinkedIn profile. Proudly display your summa, magna, and cum laude as well as valedictorian, salutatorian, or Phi Beta Kappa awards. These honors belong in the Honors and Award section and should be attached to the specific college or university by selecting the school in the drop-down menu. These awards are relevant for all ages in my opinion. Congratulations!

Professional Portfolio and Projects

Don't forget to include your professional portfolio (chapter 5) and projects from school and connect them to your university entry. (See Projects in chapter 8.)

Now let's move into several other newer profile sections that I call "credibility sections."

Resources for Chapter 7

Register at the companion website (http://www.linkedinforpersonalbranding .com) for information on the following:

- how to add, edit, or remove education information
- add or rearrange the education at the top of your profile
- how to add sections to your profile (courses and certifications)
- how to add, edit, or remove certifications

CHAPTER 8

Your Credibility Brand (Special Sections)

Are you ready for some real fun with your LinkedIn profile? My workshop students love adding in the special sections to their profiles. If you have been on LinkedIn for many years, you may not even be aware that the new sections exist since they were reconfigured just a few years ago.

In my programs, I like to call them the "credibility sections." These special sections are tremendous additions for your profile. Some of these will link to your experience or education. Let's consider each of these and how best to use them. If one or more doesn't apply to you, just skip to the next one!

Organizations

The Organizations section is an opportunity to highlight the professional associations and organizations that you're involved with. For example, you may belong to an industry association, such as the American Marketing Association or the New York Bar Association. Perhaps you belong to a local business or civic group, such as the Chamber of Commerce, Rotary Club, or BNI (Business Networking International).

Display your affiliations in the Organization section of your profile. Enter the name of the organization, your position, dates, and a brief description. Be sure to use the drop-down menu and select the company or university that you worked for while a member of the organization so that the organization links to that position on your profile.

See the organizations displayed below and on the profile for Craig Flaherty of Redniss & Mead. Craig is active in the community and his professional affiliations are in sync with his brand.

Organizations

American Society of Civil Engineers
Member
Starting September 1994

Sewer Commission, Darien
Vice Chairman
Starting December 2013

Environmental Protection Commission, Darien
Member
January 2006 – December 2012

Building Board of Appeals, Darien
Member

Vincent Van Gogh

"The key to success is for you to make a habit throughout your life of doing the things you fear."

Patents

If you are an inventor or have partnered with engineers at your company and created a patent, don't forget to add your patents to your LinkedIn profile. Add the special section called Patents. First, enter the patent office and indicate whether it's pending or issued. Then include the patent title, number, URL, description, and link to any coinventors.

Interesting Fact: More than six million patents have been issued in the United States since the first one in 1790. Do you have a patent? More important, is it on your LinkedIn profile?

Publications

The Publications section is one of my favorites because there are so many ways to use it to share your expertise and brand. Publications by or about you instill trust, credibility, and confidence.

Enter the title, publisher, description, publication dates, and any coauthors. Add a URL if the article or book is online. Here are five unique ways to use the Publications section:

1. **Articles or blogs authored by you.** If you are a prolific article writer or blogger, select the most strategic ones to highlight on your LinkedIn profile.
2. **Articles written about you or quoting or mentioning you.** Add the title, date, and a short description. Always be

clear and add the name of the article author; otherwise it's assumed that you wrote the piece. Link to the author's profile. I like to add my quote or describe how I was mentioned in the article.

3. **Your book or e-book.** Indicate date and publisher and add a description. Use the link to connect to the e-commerce site for purchase of your book, such as the Amazon page.

4. **Books by other authors.** If you are mentioned, quoted, or referenced in a book written by someone else, make sure you list the author very clearly and indicate in the description that you were quoted or mentioned. I always recommend that you link to the book or article you are referencing if it is available online. This is a great support to your author friend.

5. **Your "author pages."** This can be an Amazon page, columnist page, or a blog author page. I use this to link to all the sites where I regularly blog or share presentations.

There are many ways to use the Publications section. Select the publications that support your personal brand the best, and delete the others so your page is more personally relevant.

Here is an example from Bryan Mattimore's LinkedIn profile; Bryan is the author of three books: all of these entries link to the corresponding Amazon page.

 Publications

21 Days to a Big Idea
Diversion Books
October 17, 2015

This is a daily fitness program for the creative mind. Includes 5 creative thinking strategies and 9 personal idea generation techniques to help you create a big idea.

Idea Stormers: How to Lead and Inspire Creative Breakthroughs
Wiley Jossey- Bass
2012

For leaders of innovation teams, this is an indispensable resource for helping you to know which creative techniques to use to solve a wide variety of business challenges including: new products, positioning, strategy, packaging, promotion, and cost cutting.

99% Inspiration: Tips, tales and techniques for liberating your business creativity
Amacom
1993

A fun guide to rediscovering your creative talents. Includes a wide variety of easy to learn techniques and real world stories.

Here is an example from coauthors Mary Abbazia and Tom Spitale's profiles. Mary listed the publisher, date, title, and her coauthor on her profile. This entry links directly to their book page on Amazon.

Publications

The Accidental Marketer
Wiley
March 2014

2 authors

Mary Abbazia
Strategic Marketing Coach, Instructor, A...

Tom Spitale
Helping B2B Accidental Marketers Devel...

Languages

Add the languages that you speak and the level of proficiency. This is an important section because many people will decide to do business with you based on your ability to communicate with them in their native tongue. However, if you only speak English, I recommend that you do not indicate that as your language since it is implied.

If you are multilingual, you may want to consider creating a version of your profile in a second or third language. (See Chapter 11 for a brief description and the website for "how-to" links.)

See Felix Giannini's language entries below:

Languages

English
Native or bilingual proficiency

French
Professional working proficiency

Spanish
Elementary proficiency

Italian
Elementary proficiency

Volunteering

Are you a volunteer?

Mahatma Gandhi

"The best way to find yourself is to lose yourself in the service of others."

Prospective hiring managers, recruiters, colleagues, and business partners place value on volunteering activities. In the Volunteering section of LinkedIn, list the organization name, your role, date, and a brief description. When you enter the organization's name, you'll have the opportunity to add the logo to your profile by selecting the proper drop-down choice.

The volunteer work you do can often be a valuable reflection of your personal brand.

Here is an example: Emily Chalk, founder of East of Ellie, serves as vice president of communications for her local chapter of the International Special Events Society.

fice President of Communications, International Special Events
Society of Connecticut
nternational Special Events Society (ISES)

uly 2015

ounded more than 25 years ago with a vision to establish the live events profession as a significant
ontributor to the overall discipline of marketing and face-to-face communication.

his position provides online marketing, advertising and social media support for the Connecticut ISES
ssociation that is devoted to event professionals and members regarded as the very best in what they
o. To achieve that original vision, we continue to work diligently to ensure that our members are the
ost well connected, knowledgeable and prepared in the industry to enable them to provide the very best
ve event experiences for their clients. **less**

Related Sections

There are three other unique but closely related sections that may fit you well:

- Supported Organizations
- Causes You Care About
- Volunteering Opportunities

These optional sections are very easy to fill out by following the prompts from LinkedIn.

Honors and Awards

Take the opportunity to highlight your awards and any special recognition. Many of my clients are in sales, so there are sales awards that they are able to list on their profile. If you've been with a company for many years and received the same award every year, you may want to consolidate and list the name of the award and describe the range of years.

Industry awards are appropriate for this section. This could include recognition for a "top blog" or "top website."

Add awards you received while attending a college or university. This may include Phi Beta Kappa, cum laude, summa cum laude, magna cum laude, valedictorian, or special awards unique to your school or department.

This is also a great spot if you've received any kind of community recognition. One of my clients received the award called "40 under 40."

Note the example below of Jennifer Buchholz's awards on her LinkedIn profile: Jennifer's awards tie in directly to her personal brand. She is a powerful business leader who actively helps other women in the community. Jennifer's award section is substantial. Note that she streamlined it by consolidating her multiple GE Pinnacle Awards into one entry.

Honors & Awards

Congressman Shays for Programs in the Community to Help Disadvantaged Women
Congressman Shays on behalf of the Women's Mentoring Network
May 2005

I was recognized by Congressman Shays for programs I initiated and developed with the Women's Mentoring Organization, a not for profit which helps disadvantaged women enter into and stay in the workplace. I raised the money for, designed and ran a yoga program for the women in the program and created a partnership with the GE Women's Network and the Women's Mentoring Network where GE women raised money and provided mentoring and skill development... **more**

GE Pinnacle Award (2 Time Recipient)
General Electric

I was recognized in two separate years (and every year I was eligible) by the top level of GE's management when awarded the prestigious Pinnacle award, recognition of the top performers at GE Capital from throughout the world.

Best GE Women's Network Hub
GE Women's Network
August 2003

The hub I co-led for two years was awarded the best hub of the year out of 200 hubs. We were recognized for innovative and effective programming to help women advance in the organization. In the year we won, we conducted 70 events which included networking dinners and breakfasts, social outings, professional development workshops and volunteer work in the community.

CA Most Powerful Women
Diversity Magazine

In 2008 I was named by Diversity Magazine as one of CA's most powerful women.

Certifications

See chapter 7, "Education and Learning Brand."

Courses and Test Scores

Please see chapter 7, "Your Education and Learning Brand."

Skills

Please see chapter 10, "Skills and Social Proof."

Projects

Projects is one of my favorite sections of the LinkedIn profile. You can be extremely creative in how you use the Projects section. For myself, I have used the Projects section to list various projects or programs that I wanted to highlight.

Examples of Ways to Use the Projects Section

1. **List actual projects that are outside the scope of your normal job responsibilities.** Perhaps you serve on a technology committee at your company, for example.

2. **List specific customer projects or case studies.** These may or may not include customer names. You may need to ask permission if you do use names.
3. **Add examples of your typical work projects.** This is a creative way to describe the work you do.

Many of my clients and friends will use these in very innovative ways. You may want to use the Project section to describe customer projects specifically and link to the website page. Conversely, you can describe the project without using a customer name.

Steve Gardiner, president of Gardiner Associates, uses the Project section of his LinkedIn profile very creatively. He lists two of his most strategic projects. The first one is Steve's "Grounded Leadership Profiles" and the second is "The Leadership Forum at Silver Bay." He includes a comprehensive write up for both projects, but his Silver Bay story is the most magical. Silver Bay is the country's longest-running leadership conference, and Steve tells his personal story about his family's Silver Bay traditions. Three generations of leadership!

In this example below, Felix Giannini lists his projects by client name and description. These projects are linked to his role at Lexco Inc.

 Projects

MCI International Headquarters and 2 Satellite Facilities - Security
1982 – 1985

Created written and plan specifications in conjunction with project architect and engineering companies. Project managed entire system installation and commissioning, for security and life safety systems valued at over $1.5 million. This work included the Western Union International Building in Manhattan.

Pitney Bowes Corporate Headquarters and 9 Satellite Facilities - Security
1983 – 1993

Created written and plan security system specifications for a company wide integrated security program in conjunction with the project architect and engineering companies. Project managed entire security system installation and commissioning. Consulted on the security and life safety systems management polices and procedures. Total security projects valued at over 10 million dollars.

EF Hutton World Headquarters: Complete Building Security
January 1985 – January 1988

Created written and plan specifications for building wide security systems in conjunction with project architect and engineering companies. Project managed entire security system installation and commissioning. Security and life safety systems valued at over 2 million dollars.

Columbia University Faculty Housing Buildings
1989 – 1991

Created written and plan specifications in conjunction with project architect and engineering companies. Project managed entire system installation and commissioning, for security and life safety systems valued at over 2 million dollars.

Here's what to include in the Projects section: Include the project name, date, team members, and description. Be sure to link it to your occupation with the drop-down menu. The other great thing about the Projects section is that you are able to add a URL and link to a webpage. Include other team members to your projects. Remember to link to your Experience or Education sections using the drop-down menu.

Always think of your personal brand when it comes to deciding which projects to highlight. If they are outside of your brand mission, just leave them off. I am continually adding, deleting, and prioritizing the projects.

Advice for Contacting

This is one of my very favorite sections, which we discussed in chapter 3.

Personal Sections

What about the Personal section? Using this section is your own decision, but I really do like the "interests" area because it helps you to connect with others in a more personal way. Indicate if you love golf, tennis, watching sports, cooking, or walking dogs. Some of my clients are practicing for a marathon, beekeeping, writing a blog, or dancing for charity.

We all love to learn about the human interest side of a person, so why not bring that out a little bit in this section of your profile? Remember people hire people. People buy from people. This is the one small area where your personal hobbies may be a good icebreaker or connection point.

I personally don't use the Birthday and Marital Status sections. Birthday wishes are for Facebook, not LinkedIn. I did have one corporate user that loved wishing clients "happy birthday" using LinkedIn InMail, and it was very effective. Most of my clients don't do this, but you can decide what fits best for your business. And there are certainly LinkedIn users who wish to display "married" on their profile. My advice is either show "married" or show nothing at all.

Marie Patel shares her personal interests with a flair:

Additional Info

• Interests

World Traveler, Golfer, Mom Taxi, Spin and Yoga Enthusiast

The credibility sections are a tremendous way to build on your personal brand with very specific examples and links. Next stop is the very strategic and important chapter 9. We are now ready to discuss the LinkedIn Summary and headline.

Resources for Chapter 8

Appendix C, for character counts and specifications

Register at the companion website (http://www.linkedinforpersonalbranding .com) for information on the following:

- how to add sections to your profile

CHAPTER 9

Your Strategic Headline and Summary

It's time to put on your "strategy hat." A professional photo, headline, and summary have the greatest impact on the effectiveness of your LinkedIn profile for your personal branding.

These three sections are setting the stage for your profile viewers.

It is at this point where your reader will decide if he or she wishes to learn more about you. **Photo. Summary. Headline.**

We discussed the headshot photo in chapter 5. In this chapter, we will be reviewing the professional headline and summary.

LinkedIn Professional Headline

Your headline and photo are often the only things your prospect sees before deciding to click on your profile. For those of you that are actively working to get more career or sales inquiries, consider creating a compelling keyword rich headline. (See chapter 4 to learn about researching keywords.)

The headline is powerful for two reasons. First, it is significant from a search perspective. The keywords that you select for your headline could be the very words that help a client, prospect, recruiter, or hiring manager find you.

Secondly, and really just as important, the headline creates an immediate first impression of you. The viewer sees your partial profile (headshot and headline) and will subsequently make a split-second decision about whether to look at your profile or skip to the next more interesting person. You want your headline to be interesting, compelling, and authentic.

You choose the words for your LinkedIn headline and they will appear near your headshot at the top. Many people don't realize that there is a default setting within LinkedIn. Your latest title from the Experience section is the automatic default headline if you make no adjustments to the settings.

The headline space is very generous. There are 120 very valuable characters available to you. If you use a list of keywords, separate them with a comma or a pipe character. Think about what you want people to think of you and what you want to be found for.

Top Ten Headline Creation Tips

1. **Be strategic.** Focus on your top priorities. Keep your headline and summary in sync with each other. Make sure your headline accurately reflects your personal brand and professional priorities.

2. **Use keywords and language.** Use your strategic keywords and language naturally. Refer to chapter 4 about keyword research.

3. **Consider alternative language.** Consider all the possible titles and phrases for your position and headline. Decide which goes in your headline and in your Experience section. This is especially important if you are seeking a new position. For example, a salesperson might be an account executive, sales representative, relationship manager, client manager, and so on.

3. **Add value.** Consider adding in a short benefit or value statement in your LinkedIn headline. You can add this after keywords or in place of them.

4. **Be truthful.** Make sure when you create your headline that it does match your brand and is very truthful. Don't ever change a manager to a vice president or coordinator to manager anywhere on your profile page.

5. **Jazz it up.** You might decide to choose the words "professional," "executive," or "enthusiast" instead of "specialist" or "associate." I am not personally comfortable with "ninja," "guru," "wizard," or "superstar" in a headline, but you can decide that for yourself.

6. **Be specific.** This will help draw more favorable attention to your expertise. Headlines that are very generic and often overused are as follows: account executive, project manager, consultant, and analyst. Consider adding words to differentiate yourself from all the other account executives or project managers.

7. **Be mindful of the company you keep.** Consider your corporate brand. If you are currently a "senior VP at GE" or a "managing director at JLL," then I suggest you retain that powerful corporate branding in your personal headline. The company brand will attract viewers to your page.

8. **Name drop.** If you have appeared in the media or have other high-profile exposures, consider mentioning this in a headline (e.g., "Forbes contributor").

9. **Compare.** Look at others in your industry for ideas and language.

10. **Be comfortable with your headline.** If it doesn't feel right to you, change it immediately.

Examples

Old headline	Marketing Manager
New headline	Marketing Executive	Growth Strategy	Channel Development	Partner Relations
Old headline	Human Resources Consultant
New headline	Human Resources Consultant	HR	Talent Acquisition	Employee Retention	Optimizing Your Workforce for Growth
Old headline	Operations Manager
New headline	Operations Manager	Call Center Optimization	Black Belt	Six Sigma	Military Veteran
Old headline	Financial Analyst
New headline	Financial Analyst Specializing in Audit, Risk and Compliance
Old headline	CFO
New headline	CFO	Chief Financial Officer	Delivering Profitable Growth Strategies
Old headline	Student at University of Michigan
New headline	MBA Candidate University of Michigan, Class of 2016	Operations and Leadership

For Employees

Think about the company that employs you when crafting your headline. If you are a salesperson for a company, you might want to first list the title and company name and then add keywords or describe how you bring value to clients. There are many ways and opportunities to have a compelling headline. Consider your personal brand and also your company's goals and culture.

For Team Leaders and Company Executives

At our Post Road Consulting workshops, we work on LinkedIn personal branding with many teams and companies. We typically create a few choices of headlines that incorporate the company or team name and also allow for some personal differentiation. We may suggest that the employee display the job title and company, especially with a recognizable company brand, but this is up to our client. In other instances, we create several value statements for the headlines and the employees choose the one they prefer.

For Job Seekers

It's usually best not to say "unemployed" or "searching" in your headline. Instead, use your strategic keywords and a value statement. If you are a military veteran, add "military veteran" to your headline.

Old headline	Unemployed Seeking Marketing Role
New headline	Marketing Leader ∣ Digital Media ∣ Lead Generation Specialist ∣ Military Veteran

Author's Headline

I am an owner of a small business called Post Road Consulting LLC. It was more important for me to use keywords and language that people can associate with my brand than it is to be "owner of Post Road Consulting LLC." Perhaps as my company grows, I will decide to rethink my LinkedIn headline. Truth be told, I am always tinkering with it and updating my headline.

For my current headline, I use keywords and a value proposition:

Sandra Long: Current Headline
LinkedIn Speaker ∣ LinkedIn Trainer ∣ Social Selling ∣ Personal Brandingl Jumpstart your business, brand and career
vs.
Owner Post Road Consulting LLC

Real Headline Examples from a Few Clients and Friends

KEYWORD FOCUS

Felix Giannini: President of Lexco Inc.
Security and Fire Alarm Engineering / Business Continuity Planning / Thought Leader / Expert Witness / Speaker / Veteran

VALUE FOCUS

Mary Beth Moran Nelsen: President of The Right Resource
I help people and businesses develop productive communication skills.

VALUE FOCUS

Kathy McShane: CEO and Founder of Ladies Launch Club
Making entrepreneurship available to all women.

Your headline choice is ultimately your decision. It is your personal headline, not necessarily your job title—but it might be. Will you be "marketing manager at ABC Company," or will you be an "online marketing and social media expert"? Will you be "president of XYZ Solutions," or will you be "innovator ∣ entrepreneur ∣ technology." You can also consider doing both.

Use your title and then add a jazzy list of keywords or a benefit statement. All of this will depend on your industry and personal style.

Whatever your situation, take your time to really think about the best headline for you. What would work best with your industry and prospects?

LinkedIn Summary

Your LinkedIn summary is valuable digital real estate. You are allotted two thousand characters to tell the right story to help you attract the perfect client or job. Be sure not to just rehash what is already in your profile, such as where you work or went to school.

Try to weave together your story in an interesting way to compel your audience to be motivated to work with you or refer you to someone else. This is especially important to do if you have a disjointed work history.

Sandra's Ten Favorite Tips for a LinkedIn Summary

There are many ways to write your summary. Here are overall principles of how to succeed with a LinkedIn summary:

1. **Like it.** If you aren't comfortable with it, rewrite it. Make it something you are extremely comfortable with.
2. **Set goals.** First consider your goals. What are you trying to achieve with your summary and profile in general? Are you a job seeker or recruiter? Are you trying to find new partners? Are you trying to make a sale or get a new prospect? Are you trying to highlight your expertise for potential partners or speaking venues?
3. **Consider your readers.** Think about all your "audiences," such as current colleagues, candidates, past coworkers, future employers or customers, neighbors, and friends. Consider your audiences and how you can help them. What will make the reader want to read all of your profile and to contact you for more?
4. **Use the space.** There are two thousand characters available. I have a few clients who only want a short summary, and that is OK because it fits them. But don't just give up because it's hard to write about yourself. This space is a golden opportunity for the "preselling" of your personal brand. In fact, LinkedIn reported that a summary of at least forty words makes your profile more likely to be found in search.
5. **Be true and genuine.** It should reflect the real "you" as a worker, leader, recruiter, sales person, colleague, volunteer, and so on.

6. **Make it compelling with first person.** Use first person to create more warmth with your reader. Are you sharing something personal or unique that differentiates you against your competitors? Does your personality come through? (Refer back to chapter 4 as you consider this.)

On August 3, 2016, LinkedIn reported that 40 percent of recruiters are looking for some evidence of personality from a candidate's profile.

---

7. **Consider language.** Use the words that you wish to be known and found for in your summary. Make sure it all sounds natural and authentic. At the end of your summary, you may want to list out the specialties in a list. Some of your readers will prefer to read a list, and it is another chance to use your keywords.
8. **Use an attractive layout.** Make sure your profile has an appealing layout. You are somewhat limited by LinkedIn's editing features in this section, but you can use spacing, capitalization, and symbols in your profile to make it more attractive. For example, you can capitalize a paragraph heading to make it stand out more prominently.
9. **Start strong.** Start with an interesting hook for an opening sentence and paragraph. This may be a question or an authentic opening. Draw your reader in with your own story at the beginning of your summary.
10. **Close carefully.** Add a specialties list and contact information at the end of the summary. I like the list because it adds keywords and it gives an alternate "quick read" for your viewers. Some people will never want to bother with a paragraph, so include both a paragraph and a brief list. (Attorneys should never use the word "specialty" or "specialties.") Add your contact info at the end of your summary.

LinkedIn Summary: Personas

There are many different ways that you can use this valuable real estate to share your personal brand on LinkedIn. I have identified several types of summary personas that I'd like to share with you. These personas can help you think through how you might express yourself on your LinkedIn summary. Think of the approach and structure that appeals to you. Read through these and see if one of these resonates with you and helps tell your story.

The Historian

The historian format is probably the most common on LinkedIn. With this format, a chronological list of experience and education is commonly recalled. One of the problems I see is that many historians tend to repeat exactly what is listed in their LinkedIn profile sections. They identify their college, where they work, what years, and so on. So in that sense, oftentimes, historians are wasting the opportunity of a LinkedIn summary. It may be factual, but it's boring!

If you want to be a historian, make sure to add a glimpse of your personality or your values. Let some of "you," the person, shine through somewhere. Consider all the elements of a personal brand we listed in chapter 2, and decide if you want some of those more intangible aspects to shine through to differentiate yourself. Or consider the opportunity to take your history and turn it into more of a story, if at all possible. Bring your history to life in a more interesting way in your summary!

The Storyteller

If you have a great story that fits in with your personal brand or highlights you in a special way, you may want to use a story format. Use a great opening sentence. Start at the beginning of the story, and tell it just like you would tell your friend. In a way, I think that all of the summaries should read or open like a story if possible.

In my own LinkedIn summary, I talk about moving around the northeastern United States with my family as I was growing up. This shaped my perspective on first impressions and managing (personal branding) and meeting people and making friends (building a network).

As part of our True North Personal Branding[SM] at Post Road Consulting, our team encourages clients to figure out a way to tell their own story. It is absolutely fascinating. We all ended up where we are today as a result of some story. Here are a few examples:

- Corporate real estate executive Michael A. started his career on a golf course (from caddy to executive).
- Bank leader Valerie Senew describes growing up in an entrepreneurial family and how that helps her as a small business banker.
- Civil engineer Jorge Pereira starts his LinkedIn summary saying that he is "the son of a carpenter" and how that led him to engineering.
- Corporate real estate financial analyst Neil E. shares his early career story of studying and working in China. Ultimately, Neil joins a top corporate real estate company and describes how he applies his knowledge to the global clients his company serves.

- Keynote speaker and author (*Politics of Promotion*) Bonnie Marcus tells the story of being witness to exceptional women in the workplace who faced barriers.

The Weaver

The weaver format is very important for people who have not had a linear career trajectory. These are the folks that have done multiple things in multiple industries and maybe even across multiple geographies. If you looked at just their experience sections on their LinkedIn profile, you would be confused. You would think: "What's this person all about? What does he or she want to do? Why is he or she doing this or that?"

Use the summary section to effectively connect the dots. Explain why these various positions made sense for you, what they have in common, or what you learned from this unusual path. Weave it all together into a coherent and meaningful story.

If you have a nonlinear career, it is especially interesting if you can effectively weave your story together. For example, you may want to explain why you began a corporate career and then transitioned to start your own firm. Or perhaps you describe why you went back to get school to get your MBA. Or you explain how you are able to run two businesses or play in a band on the weekends. What brought you to this point? Why did you become interested in law or business or the arts?

This type of format is very useful in explaining your new role. I used this format myself for a few years. I spent thirty-plus years in a sales leadership role at a large company. Then I left to start my own business. My profile summary at that time had to start out with a "weaver" component. I wanted to explain how that role prepared me for my new company, so I wove together the story.

Here is a great weaver example:

Summary Sample: Amy Krompinger, "Weaver" and "Storyteller"

I have an entrepreneurial spirit that I have developed through my work as an HR leader and a small business owner. I love taking my ideas and working to make them a reality. As a multifaceted professional, I leverage my business knowledge with strategy and people to be successful.

Growing up in Delaware and playing field hockey throughout my youth, I acquired a strong love for the game. So much so, that I played for the D1 team at UCONN. While at UCONN, I not only fed my love for field hockey, but also for business and communications. When it came time to pick a career, I knew I wanted to be in business with an emphasis on people, so HR was a natural fit.

Once I graduated, I couldn't leave the field hockey aspect completely at UCONN, so I started to coach for various teams and club. After some time, I realized that there was space and need in the market for me to start a club field hockey team unlike the others in the state. So, that's what I did.

Specialties

- Social Recruiting
- Performance Management
- Coaching
- Training
- Onboarding
- Collaborating with business partners
- Business strategy

Personality: Ambitious, Strategic, Sociable

Contact

Aim Athletes LLC. ✉: aimathletes@gmail.com
Affinion Group ✉: akrompinger@affiniongroup.com

The Themer

The themer format is very helpful for senior-level executives or people with a range of experience. If you have enjoyed a long career, and you have accomplished quite a few things, your experience can appear to be overwhelming. It often makes sense to clarify and fine tune those very special attributes or themes that you want to accentuate.

The themer format is also very appropriate for people with a nonlinear career. Identify the most significant elements to emphasize in your summary. One of the best ways to do that is to pick three or four themes. These are themes that have permeated your career across all of your different positions and experiences. You may have had different jobs and different experiences, whether they are professional experiences within organizations or volunteering, but these are themes that are important to you and best reflect your personal brand.

The themer persona is particularly effective for senior leaders like Lisa Bonner from Hartford, Connecticut. Lisa's experience *themes* are clearly described in her summary below:

I am a change agent and thrive in and drive an environment of organizational transformation. I leverage courageous leadership, innovation, and technology to create sustainable behavior change, making it possible for companies to outperform in this new reality. I have learned that the most successful path is a collaborative one, so I surround myself with talented colleagues, develop strong relationships with my business partners, and empower accountability. My focus areas:

CHANGE MANAGEMENT—ORGANIZATION TRANSFORMATION: Develop and implement effective change management strategies to lift business performance.

Engage employees and build capabilities to create sustainable behavior change. Certified in Prosci® ADKAR® change management methodology.

ENTERPRISE COLLABORATION AND COMMUNICATION—SOCIAL MEDIA: Strong track record in utilizing enterprise collaboration tools and social media to expand knowledge sharing and employee engagement, resulting in increased productivity and innovation.

REVERSE MENTORING AND MULTI-GENERATIONAL WORKPLACE: Pair early career talent with senior executives to build awareness and understanding of social media, emerging technologies and trends, enabling executives to become more fluent in digital and mobile computing and creating a competitive advantage for the organization.

LEADERSHIP DEVELOPMENT: Develop Cigna leaders with in-depth business knowledge who drive innovation. Orchestrated CIMA's Extended Leadership Conferences to deliver business value, driving personal accountability and embracing change. Moderator for enterprise-wide "Lean In Circles."

I enjoy speaking at international conferences on branding, employee engagement, reverse mentoring, enterprise collaboration, the emerging workplace, remote work and multi-generations in the work place.

Specialties

- Change Management
- Enterprise Collaboration
- Remote Work and Flexible Work Arrangements
- Driving Team Performance and Coaching

Contact

Lisa.Bonner@xxx.com

The Personality

Share your personality and how you work. This type of summary can be highly effective and interesting. Not everyone can pull off the "personality" persona. First of all, you have to really know yourself.

TIP: Don't just say you have a special type of personality. Demonstrate it with a story or your unique perspective or approach that shows your personality. Say what you love!

Notice how Emily tells her story and then shares her personality at the end of her summary.

Summary Sample: Emily Chalk, "Story Teller" and "Personality"

I began my career in the experiential marketing world organizing events for Fortune 500 companies and high profile clientele. After spending 6 and 1/2 years as global brand manager for Westin Hotels & Resorts, I understand the dynamics of being a global brand—and have the experience to develop on-brand events rooted in the core of any brand strategy. I thrive on executing legendary events that help our clients build their brands and meet their objectives.

The East of Ellie team is comprised of passionate party people who refuse to have a boring work day. I've been planning legendary events for Fortune 500 companies, Celebrities and Royalty since day 1.

I am truly a New Hampshire girl at heart, and am infamous for speaking a little faster than most. I have an unhealthy obsession with sticky notes, and can memorize movie lines and song lyrics in the blink of an eye.

The Business Leader

Any of the personas or formats above would work well for someone in a customer-facing role at a company. If your main viewers are prospective customers, you may want a summary that acts as a preselling document. It's best if you write this in a first person.

Craig Flaherty's summary (below) is a story but also very appropriate for his role as partner at Redniss & Mead. It's personal and interesting and leads you down the path to his current leadership role.

Summary Sample: Craig Flaherty, "Storyteller" and "Business Leader"

As a child, instead of sand castles I would make sand parking lots, highways, drainage canals, and treatment plants, and I would play for hours in the mud with running hoses and damming small creeks. I spent long hours in my father's plumbing shop where the motto was "It flows downhill." After excelling in math and science I chose to pursue civil engineering at Lehigh University because it was one of the strongest programs at the school.

I found Redniss & Mead right out of school when I was looking for engineers to shadow for a few days. I've been with the firm ever since, becoming an owner in 2006. Being a part of the growth and success of a smaller company has kept my interest piqued as the job variety is wide and the scope of my professional responsibilities grew in pace with my passion and aptitude. And when a project completes I still have something physical to point to and think "I helped make that" evoking the same giddy feeling as the child playing in the sand at the beach.

At this stage in my career I leverage my experience in land use and decades working closely with distinguished Planner and company President Rick Redniss to bring a broad vision to my clients, understanding their goals and dreams and deliver them in an exceptional way. Although not certified as a planner, I have had an on the job education that has lead several of my clients to refer to me as their "Zoning Engineer." I maintain my strength in civil engineering design by mentoring our growing staff, providing oversight and quality control on their design projects.

Specialties

Zoning Analysis
Feasibility and Site Planning
Land Use Entitlements and Permitting
Design of Stormwater Collection, Conveyance and Mitigation Systems
Floodplain Compliance
Sediment and Erosion Controls
Design of Roadways, Sewers, Septic Systems and other Site Infrastructure

Contact

Redniss & Mead: c.flaherty@rednissmead.com

Other Personas to Consider

Persona	Summary ideas
Problem solver	Your approach, what problems you solve, how you are most helpful to clients, why people hire you
Visionary	What inspires you; your vision for the world, community, or industry; your unique perspective
Active job seeker	Your unique value and enthusiasm for your next role (Make sure to use your top keywords to attract recruiters.)
Sales representative	Ask a question or describe a compelling customer problem. Close with a "call to action." (Ask for a meeting or refer to your website or other action.)

Still Stuck? Can You Answer a Question?

Consider trying to answer one of these questions that may be very interesting for your summary:

- How I became an XYZ
- How I solve XYZ problem
- Why people hire me
- My clients are . . .
- How I got interested in XYZ
- How I manage XYZ and ABC together

Jog Your Thinking; Use Your Brand to Tell Your Story

Remember the following personal branding themes that you might incorporate: would you like to accentuate something on this list by demonstrating or telling a story?

Personal brand attributes	Possible LinkedIn summary topics
Experience	What you have learned to appreciate about your experience or how one thing relates to another (Weaver, Storyteller)
Skills	Skills you are developing and how you are going about it (Storyteller)
Learning	Your perspective on learning or your continuous learning goals (Themer, Storyteller)
Goals	Your career or business goal for the year
Reputation	What you are known for and where you are headed now or why you are known for something including your unique perspective (Storyteller, Themer)
Passion	Your passion for X and how that impacts your business or career outlook (Storyteller, Visionary)
Values	Your company values or your personal business values (Visionary)
Personality	Your unique personality traits
Your story	How you started (Storyteller)
Network and community	How you collaborate with others or how your network is key to your success
Vision	Your vision for your business or community or career (Visionary)
Presence and attitude	How grateful you are or how optimistic you are and why (Visionary, Storyteller)
Trust and proof	A story or a set of themes to demonstrate a trusted advisor (Storyteller, Themer)
Interests	How your interests tie in with your professional goals
Leadership and mindshare	Your thought leadership focus for this coming year or use the "Themer" persona to describe the thought leadership areas
Engagement, sharing, and etiquette	Your perspective on online networking and connecting (Problem Solver)
Unique value	Your unique combination of some of the above items that gives you a distinctive perspective

LinkedIn Summary: Format, Spacing, and Appearance

Make sure your summary looks as great as it sounds. Consider using capital letters to differentiate different sections or symbols. LinkedIn's current editing options are limited. You will want some white space to improve the overall appearance.

Strong Ending

At the end of your summary, list your "specialties" (unless you are an attorney) and your contact information again. There are a few reasons to do this:

1. It is an opportunity to use your keywords in your summary again.
2. Some of your readers will not read a paragraph and go right to a list.
3. This is a good way to summarize your strengths for the reader.
4. You want to be very easy to contact. I like to have contact information at the bottom of the summary in addition to the Contacts and Advice for Contacting sections. Make it as easy as possible to be contacted.

LinkedIn Fun Fact: "A summary of at least forty words is more likely to show up in search. Be sure to add a little personality."

LinkedIn, May 26, 2016

Your Summary and Headline: A Power Team

Now we have looked at some samples and discussed possible approaches to a summary and headline. You may actually want to do these after you fill out the rest of your profile. For many people, they need to go through the full profile and then they have a better perception of how to present the big picture in the summary and headline. In my workshops, we do the headline and summary last. Make no mistake, you can certainly write your summary and headline first or last—just don't underestimate their importance!

Now let's move on to the world of skills and social proof.

Resources for Chapter 9

Chapter 2: Your Personal Brand and Your Best Authentic Self
Chapter 4: Selecting the Right Words and Language
Appendix C, for specifications and character counts

CHAPTER 10

Skills and Social Proof

Recommendations and Endorsements

Online reviews can make the difference of your being found, hired, and trusted. It takes effort. The people in your network that have LinkedIn recommendations and endorsements have worked at it. This online peer validation generally doesn't materialize on your profile without some effort and attention from you.

LinkedIn has two great opportunities for you to display "social proof" from your profile. LinkedIn recommendations and endorsements are both misunderstood and very sought after at the same time. Let's start with skills and endorsements.

Pick the Right Skills First

The first thing you need to do is select the "right" skills so you will be endorsed for the things that really matter to your brand. If you have skills in your profile, now is the time to go in and clean them up. Yes, that's right—clean them up!

Remove any skills that are not applicable to you. If a skill is not something you do or know about, then you really don't want it on your profile. Just because someone has endorsed you for a skill, this does not mean it is right for your profile and personal brand. Also take this time to make sure you have your best strategic skills on the top of your list. The top ten skills listed on your profile should be the most strategic ones that compliment your personal brand.

Your skills list is likely to change over time so check this every few months and rearrange. LinkedIn allows you to move them around (drag) so you can easily prioritize them for your profile viewers. You can also hide them, which is an option that certain people elect based on their industry (e.g., wealth manager). Otherwise, keep your skills open for others to endorse!

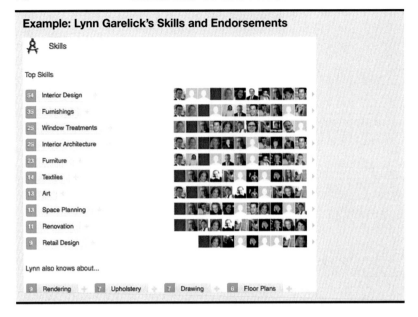

Increased Relevance of Skills and Endorsements

Despite the grumblings of some LinkedIn users, the skills and endorsements feature is becoming even more relevant over time. Recruiters and others are searching for people with specific skill sets so this adds credence to the idea of managing your skills and endorsements.

LinkedIn recently added new functionality and value to the Skills section. Find these items (with a click) that are directly related to each of your skills:

- other LinkedIn members with the same skill
- popular posts about the skill
- jobs that require the skill
- SlideShare presentations about the skill
- relevant groups

The skills are also increasingly important for recruiting purposes. The newly (2016) updated version of LinkedIn Recruiter prompts the user for skills as shown below:

LinkedIn Fun Fact: Users that display at least five relevant skills are messaged thirty-one times more and viewed seventeen times more than those that do not.

LinkedIn, August 3, 2016

What Is the "Skills Gap?"

Employers want to see more technical skills from new graduates. Increasingly, employers are seeking "soft skills" such as communication and writing.

Giving and Getting Endorsements the Right Way

Endorsements are the "one click" positive acknowledgement given to a first-level connection. I don't like the automatic endorsement suggestion messages that come directly from LinkedIn. This confuses users and causes people to endorse people they barely know. Instead, use endorsements strategically with your network.

Start by endorsing others often. Make it a routine, but always do it authentically. Endorse coworkers, customers, vendors, or anyone who has helped you, has taught you something, or has skills you can authentically vouch for.

Timing is key. Endorse someone the day he or she helped you solve a problem or the day he or she taught you a new skill. Endorse someone after a great meeting, class, or receiving advice or a favor. Definitely endorse people for skills that you know they possess.

It's smart to ask for endorsements. Do this by having a conversation with your customers, colleagues, or managers. Let them know you have rearranged and prioritized your skills on your LinkedIn profile. Just ask. Of course, it's always nice to endorse them first and discuss the skills that you both have—and skills that you are developing. It usually leads into a nice conversation about personal development and learning.

TIP: Only endorse people that you know and do so authentically for skills they possess!

Recommendations

LinkedIn recommendations provide valuable "social proof" to your network. Recommendations are personally written by your first-level connection. You approve the recommendation before it is displayed on your profile. It takes more time and thought than an endorsement. The recommendations you are given are directly associated with a specific work or educational experience.

TIP: Try to get at least three recommendations. Try to give at least five recommendations.

Make sure the recommendations you receive or write are accurate and not in violation of confidentiality. You approve and manage the display of each written recommendation on your LinkedIn profile.

Giving and receiving visible LinkedIn recommendations has helped me enormously over the years. Prospects no longer ask for "references" since I have managed all of this online. A LinkedIn recommendation is a public online validation of your work and capabilities.

In order to get the written recommendations, you will need to ask clients, partners, referral sources, and community connections. The best time to ask for a recommendation is when you are concluding a project, assignment, or job.

Best recommendations to get	Customers, direct boss, significant titles
Also good to have from	Coworkers, industry colleagues, partners
Remember to give to	Coworkers, industry colleagues, partners, employees, vendors

Getting Recommendations the Right Way

Here is my step-by-step process for asking for a recommendation:

1. **Decide who in your network can best describe your work firsthand as a result of your work together.** Make a list of possible people to ask.
2. **Always consider timing for the best results.** The best time may be just as you are finishing a project or a job with a client. Always remember to ask as you are leaving one job or project for another. Ask as soon as your client or manager gives you a big compliment.

3. **Ask for the recommendation.** If it's someone very close, you can send him or her a note or LinkedIn recommendation request. If it's someone you haven't talked to in a while, I recommend you warm him or her up a bit. Give him or her a call or meet for coffee. Tell him or her how important project X was and that you are working on your LinkedIn profile. Let him or her know that this recommendation is very important to you and appreciated. I have found that making a personalized request greatly increases your success rate.

4. **Once he or she agrees, ask how you can make it easy.** Would he or she like some ideas about what to say? Send him or her the link directly from LinkedIn.

5. **You may need to follow up with your colleague.** People often have the very best intentions but fail to complete a task. A gentle reminder is smart. Your connection may be confused on how to do it, so you may have to provide some navigational guidance.

6. **Show gratitude.** Send your friend, manager, or customer a thank-you note or InMail for their thoughtful recommendation.

TIP: Use this link to request a recommendation

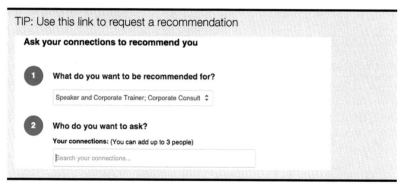

It's perfectly OK to recommend someone who recommends you. This is especially true for team situations. Why not initiate a conversation such as this after a project: "I really enjoyed working with you. We had the best team! I am very proud of our results. Let's write a LinkedIn recommendation for each other based on this great achievement"

A June 2016 study conducted by Post Road Consulting LLC determined that 54 percent of LinkedIn users consider LinkedIn recommendations either "very or moderately important" to their career and personal brand.

Giving

Writing recommendations for others is as valuable as receiving them yourself. For leaders, they are even more important. Be sure to be generous by giving authentic recommendations to people who have worked for you as an employee, partner, or vendor. Remember to give recommendations to your colleagues and coworkers. Well-written specific recommendations reflect positively on the writer and the recipient.

Giving recommendations and endorsements is just as important as getting them! There are so many reasons. Here are a few of my favorites:

- It's the right thing to do! If you really appreciate someone's work then support him or her with an endorsement or recommendation. Simple.
- You are a leader or mentor. You encourage, support, and help others as a leader. If I see a leader who doesn't give recommendations, it just doesn't look right. This is especially true if I see a leader who has received but not given.
- You will be noticed on the page of the person you are recommending. You will be seen on the page of the superstar you endorsed or recommended.
- Giving often prompts getting. And that is OK, as long as the endorsements and recommendations are meaningful and genuine.

How to Give

The mechanics are simple. Go directly to your colleague's profile to recommend him or her. However, it usually makes sense to discuss the recommendation first. Make sure you are mentioning what is most important—and usually he or she can guide you a little bit.

Your colleagues, team, and vendors will be delighted if you give them a genuine endorsement or recommendation. Figure out which one is most suitable for the situation. Your vendors, colleagues, and team will appreciate a written recommendation but it might not be suitable for your customer or manager. Use an endorsement for that situation. There's no reason not to endorse a customer or manager as long as it's authentic.

The best recommendations are specific and timely. Saying "She's a true professional" is usually not as meaningful as describing a specific situation with details.

TIP: You manage your recommendations. You choose which ones to accept and display.

Here are examples of four recommendations that I have given over the years:

My Recommendation for Lisa Bernard—I Heard Lisa Speak and Bought Her Workbook

Lisa is an exceptional speaker, writer, coach and consultant. I have learned so much from her speaker-oriented training and workbook. Lisa is extremely insightful and helpful. I am now reconfiguring many of my practices and presentations as a result of Lisa's advice. For anyone that strives to be the very best in the world of speaking, I highly recommend Lisa Bernard.

My Recommendation for David Czarneski—Previous Coworker

David is an incredibly talented operations leader and executive. I worked with him at PBMS for a few years when he was managing the Windsor facility and several significant customer contracts. David's word is gold. He makes all the right things happen for his customers and is very modest in regards to taking credit for himself. David Czarneski is a highly respected business leader and I hope to someday have the chance to work with him again (or refer business to him).

My Recommendation for Lisa Bonner—Previous Customer, Current Mentor and Friend

Lisa Bonner is a captivating, intelligent, and articulate speaker. I heard Lisa speak at both Working Mother Social Media conferences in NYC (2012 and 2013) and was highly impressed each time. Lisa has a unique ability to simultaneously share information and inspire the audience. Her expertise in change management, workplace best practices, and reverse mentoring provides fascinating content for her sessions. I highly recommend and endorse Lisa Bonner.

My Recommendation for Aneta Hall—Previous Coworker

Aneta Hall is a lady with tremendous capabilities and potential. In my view, she is a social media rock star that has brought great marketing savvy to PB. Aneta has greatly enhanced the PB social media presence over the past couple of years. Now she is sharing the knowledge across the company with excellent training and guidance. Her program is empowering others! I feel fortunate to work with someone like Aneta Hall and highly recommend her.

Your recommendations and endorsements will reflect directly on your personal brand. They are the best forms of "social proof." Spend the time to work on these to benefit your network and yourself. Now let's turn our attention to your company matters.

Note for wealth management professionals: endorsements can be easily turned off. See resource links below.

Resources for Chapter 10

Register at the companion website (http://www.linkedinforpersonalbranding .com) for information on the following:

- how to add or remove skills
- how to rearrange the display order of your skills
- how to hide or unhide skills
- requesting a recommendation
- editing or removing recommendations
- how to recommend others
- visibility of recommendations on your profile
- accepting and displaying recommendations on your profile

CHAPTER 11

Profile Appearance and Final Check

If you've come this far, you are now ready to think about the final touches including appearance, consistency, and confidentiality. Simply loading in the information and images is not enough. You want to make your profile meaningful and attractive. There are several ways to do this.

Have a Consistent Personal Brand on LinkedIn

If you are displaying too many different and unrelated skills and experiences, your brand will be confusing. Too much information can sometimes hurt your positioning. Remove anything that is totally irrelevant to your brand and priorities. The same can be said for status updates. Keep the majority of your updates and likes centered on your brand and those that support your network.

Be Strategic with the Order of Your Profile Sections

That's right—put your most important sections near the top. Always remember your personal brand as the guidepost of where you rearrange your various sections. Many of your profile viewers will not make it all the way through to the end. Here are a few examples of logical section rearrangements:

- Author moves Publications to the top position after Summary.
- New financial advisor moves Certifications above Volunteering, Organizations, Interests, Advice for Contacting, and Education.
- Community volunteer moves Volunteering to the top after Summary.

- New graduate without substantial work experience moves Education to the top position after Summary.

Confidentiality Can Affect Your Brand

Now's the time to double-check that you have not shared any confidential information on your LinkedIn profile. We discussed this earlier as we reviewed the Experience section. Take another look over the entire profile to be sure. Confidentiality is that important!

Check for Technical Accuracy and Consistency

Your profile is your responsibility, even if you hired someone to help you write your profile or résumé. You are the one who will approve all content. There are several ways to check it:

- Make sure your profile dates are consistent with your résumé. Some recruiters will immediately disregard a candidate with inconsistent dates.
- Use the same type of bullet point (or colon or dash) throughout.
- Be consistent with how you start and end sentences that are part of a list. For example, start them all with a present or past action verb and end them all with a period (or not).
- Remove anything that is not 100 percent true. Enough said.
- Check the language throughout. Be consistent with tenses. Don't mix third person and first person in your profile.
- Check the general readability of your sections.
- You may want to run your paragraphs through software to check your spelling and/or grammar. Do this first and then "copy and paste" over to LinkedIn.
- Have a good friend do a read through for an accuracy check. He or she might see something that you miss.

Remove Any and All Duplicate Profiles

Search for your name in LinkedIn to make sure there aren't any duplicate profiles on display. You don't want people finding that old profile you haven't updated in five years.

TIP: When you look at your profile, it goes into an automatic "Edit" mode. To view your profile as others do, click on the blue box labeled "View Profile As."

Format and Appearance Is a Reflection of Your Brand Too

Some of the sections are lengthy, particularly the Summary and Experience sections. Consider the overall appearance and readability. The following are examples of what to avoid:

- one huge paragraph with no breaks or bullets
- too many bullet points
- no white space
- unattractive spacing

LinkedIn does not allow for bold, italics or underlining so make good use of white space, bullets, and capital letters.

Consider Using Symbols, Capital Letters, and White Space

I like to see a summary that is very attractively laid out with clearly differentiated sections. If you have two or three distinct topics or themes in your profile, consider using capital letters as a heading. Don't use all caps because they are symbolic of shouting online.

For your bullet points, consider using symbols to make the points more interesting and distinct. Here are some examples:

For bullets you can use the following:

► ► ■ ❖ ▦ ⭑ ✔ ✗

Other symbols you can use for phone and e-mail are as follows:

✆ ☏ ☎ ✉

Find your own symbols and apply them directly or copy and paste them over to LinkedIn. Feel free to find several symbols on my LinkedIn Profile (under Projects). Just copy and paste them over to your profile, or find the symbols on the companion website.

Symbols for Your Headline

Use a comma or the vertical pipeline separator (sometimes called a pipe or vertical pipeline) symbol to separate phrases in a headline. On many keyboards, this is located above the return key on the same key as the backslash.

\ for the backslash
Shift + | for the pipe separator

Use symbols sparingly and professionally. They can make your profile much easier to read, but you don't want to overdo them.

Check Out Your Profile on Your Mobile Devices

Be sure to check how your profile renders on your tablet and mobile devices. You might want to adjust things accordingly. For example, your mobile profile only shows the top four skills so make sure those are the best ones for your brand.

Display a LinkedIn Profile Link or Badge

Add a badge or URL link from your e-mail signature, online biography, or website that goes directly to your LinkedIn profile or company page. Use every online opportunity to connect your clients, readers, or partners to your LinkedIn accounts.

Consider a "Declutter" Strategy for Your Personal Brand

If you have an exceptionally long profile, you may want to consider a decluttering strategy. This is another cleanup type decision that reflects your personal brand. Please refer to my profile (Sandra Long) for a blog post titled "Declutter Your LinkedIn Profile: Clarify Your Strategy and Brand." That post includes some of the very specific ways I was able to streamline my own profile.

Consider a Multilingual Profile

LinkedIn supports twenty-four languages. You may benefit by having a multilingual profile. The advantage is that both of your profiles will show up in a Google search with unique URLs. Your viewer can select which language to read for your profile. Creating a second or third profile will require you to input all the content a second or third time. Your profiles will be linked for ease of use. Use the drop-down menu at the top of your profile to create the new profile version.

Keep All Industry Regulations in Mind

Some regulated industries will require that you hold your LinkedIn profile to a different standard. Examples of this are wealth managers, financial advisors, and attorneys. It is your obligation to follow your industry standards. Some companies require approvals for personal summaries. Often times, the regulators require that the endorsements and recommendations be turned off. Attorneys are not supposed to use the word "specialties." If you are in a regulated industry, find out if there are special requirements for you to follow. This is your responsibility no matter who you hire for assistance.

Religion and Politics

I advise my workshop clients not to post views that pertain to religion and politics. It's certainly important to list the church, synagogue, government, or political office where you work. It's quite another thing to post religious or political views on your home feed or as a blog post. I have seen some over-the-top posts that are very controversial. Think before you post, and you should be fine.

TIP: Check your writing, spelling, and grammar. Save your changes. Have a friend give you feedback on your profile.

Keep Current

Your personal brand is always evolving, assuming you are always learning and changing. Keep your LinkedIn profile up to date at all times. Don't let it go and be in the situation like one of my clients named Lisa.

Lisa knew people were looking at her profile every day. She ignored it for two years. Out of embarrassment, she put this as her headline on LinkedIn—"profile under construction"—and left that message on her profile for two years!

When she came to me, she was desperate for a new profile. Don't get yourself in that situation by always staying attentive to your brand and your LinkedIn profile.

Resources for Chapter 11

Appendix C, for character counts and image specifications
Chapter 5: Your Visual Brand: Images, Rich Media, and Links

Register at the companion website (http://www.linkedinforpersonalbranding .com) for information on the following:

- how to rearrange profile sections
- how to change the order of positions, education, and publications within your profile
- how to change the current, previous, and education lines at the top of your profile
- how to create or delete a profile in another language
- how to close or merge a duplicate account
- how to edit your profile from a mobile device
- display a link or badge to your LinkedIn account
- symbols to copy

More Brand Matters

CHAPTER 12

Your Company Matters

For Employees and Company Leaders

Your personal brand is intertwined with your company brand, and it's particularly evident on the LinkedIn platform. This chapter is designed to apply to

- **company employees** who want to build internal and external influence and relationships;
- **senior executives** at a company or organization who want to build influence as a social leader; and
- **business owners** or leaders who want to leverage social media for the company to grow the business and brand.

As you consider and develop your personal brand on LinkedIn, keep the following in mind:

- your employer's brand as it relates to both marketing and recruiting
- the personal brands of your employees or coworkers
- the personal brands of industry colleagues

Thirteen Power Tips for Employees

You may be joining LinkedIn as an employee of a company. Is your company social media savvy—especially in relation to using LinkedIn properly? Many companies are discovering that there is a lot to learn and teach their employees.

Here are some general tips suitable for all employees:

1. **Your landscape.** Follow your company's social media feeds and blogs. Read and follow your company's social media

policy. Learn best practices and etiquette for online networking in general. Understand and follow any specific regulations regarding marketing and social media that is particular to your industry or business or department. Ask your department manager about his or her strategy.

2. **Keywords and language.** Look at your company website for marketing language that would fit in with your profile and support your brand. Find out if your company shares marketing assets for your use, such as profile examples or sample headlines. Be in sync with your company's brand messaging whenever it makes sense for you and your role.

3. **Links and rich media.** Add the company website and address to the Contact Information section of your profile. Display company-sponsored YouTube videos or SlideShare presentations on your profile, especially as it relates to your position. (See chapter 5.)

4. **Company logo.** Make sure your profile is linked to your company's LinkedIn company page and is displaying the company logo. (See mine below and refer again to chapter 6.)

 Experience

LinkedIn Speaker, LinkedIn Corporate Trainer, Sales Leader, Personal Branding, Social Selling
Post Road Consulting LLC
August 2013 – Present (2 years 10 months) | Westport CT

5. **Sharing.** Like and share company provided content on LinkedIn and elsewhere. Find it in your home feed or go directly to your company's page on LinkedIn. Some companies will e-mail content directly to employees for sharing, so don't be afraid to click and share what they send you. (See chapter 15 for detailed information on sharing content.)

6. **External influence.** Connect with key industry leaders, clients, and partners. You are the face for your company. Your personal brand reflects on your company brand! Consider showing support with likes, comments, and @mentions as appropriate.

7. **Internal influence.** Connect with coworkers. Support them by liking, sharing, or commenting on appropriate content on LinkedIn. Mention your colleague or customer name with the LinkedIn mention feature for public recognition to your networks.

TIP: Try a LinkedIn Mention. Enter the @ symbol followed by the name you are mentioning. Select the name in the drop-down.

8. **Influencers.** If someone on the leadership team in your company is actively publishing articles on LinkedIn, follow him or her and consider liking his or her articles. Find other appropriate industry partners or leaders who are influencers to follow.

9. **Groups.** Join any LinkedIn Groups managed or sponsored by your company. Join groups where your customers spend time. Listen to the conversations for great learning. Engage with helpfulness but not overt salesmanship as a member of a LinkedIn Group. (See chapter 13.)

10. **Introductions.** Connect and proactively introduce your coworkers and clients to valuable industry connections. Use LinkedIn search functions to identify the best introduction opportunities.

11. **Training.** Take LinkedIn or social media training offered by your company. Participate in company social media events or meet-ups.

12. **Teamwork.** Connect and meet with the marketing professionals at your company to let them know you are an active social media supporter. Let them know your ideas for great content and how you can help them. Get their advice on how you can enhance your presence or that of the company.

13. **Social proof.** Recommend and endorse your colleagues and partners. Do this authentically for great work results, and it will be appreciated. (See chapter 10.)

Company Executives and Leaders: "Be a Social Leader"

Company leaders have the added responsibility to support employee efforts on LinkedIn to help drive sales and recruit talent. You can and should help create and build the tools, resources, and culture to make social media successful at your organization.

- **Strategy.** Help your marketing, sales, and HR team's efforts to create a social media strategy that is focused on attracting customers and candidates.
- **Policy and plan.** Make sure your company has a clear social media policy and plan for employees. This policy needs to reflect specific industry regulations.
- **Your personal brand.** Have a complete, professional, and up-to-date LinkedIn individual profile at all times. Consider your personal brand and thought leadership goals because your customers, prospects, and potential candidates will be looking at your profile.

- **Your thought leadership brand.** Are you a speaker or presenter? Consider uploading videos and presentations to your personal profile or linking with YouTube and SlideShare content. Consider blogging on the LinkedIn Publisher platform. This is one of the most powerful ways to share your thought leadership and personal brand. (See chapter 14.)
- **Leadership with internal influence.** Leverage your employee base to assist marketing and HR to attract customers and candidates. Your actions will make an enormous impact on your team's effective adoption of social media for sales and talent acquisition. Connect with coworkers and support their LinkedIn activities and posting.
- **External influence.** Connect with all of your company's best clients, prospects, and partners as a starting point. Create a networking strategy to connect and meet with industry leaders and prospects. Use LinkedIn to bridge over to meaningful live face to face meetings.
- **Generous leadership.** Recommend and endorse employees and partners when appropriate. This is an excellent reflection of your brand and values.
- **Brand ambassadors.** Consider professional training and photographic headshots for your employee teams. Your employees are the best extension of your company brand. Their online presence amplifies your company's brand with clients, prospects, and candidates.
- **Advanced needs.** Consider the special needs of your salespeople and recruiters. LinkedIn offers a license for recruiters called "Recruiter" and one for sales personnel called "Sales Navigator." Make sure your team is well trained in order to leverage both the free and premium platforms from LinkedIn. Assign an internal or external resource to monitor licenses and drive results.
- **Company page.** Make sure your marketing team has created a LinkedIn company page. They should be posting content that is interesting and helpful to customers, prospects, candidates, and partners.
- **Investing in the company page.** Consider premium versions or features for your LinkedIn company page for your HR and marketing team. Your company can advertise to a targeted prospect list, post jobs, or display a career page.

Case Study: Personal Branding for a Company

More and more companies are investing in personal branding with LinkedIn for their employees. Redniss & Mead is a civil engineering firm in Stamford, Connecticut. The firm made the decision to conduct four LinkedIn personal branding "hands-on" workshops for employees. For Redniss & Mead, it was a valuable exercise because the firm recognizes that employees are the best brand ambassadors. Clients, prospects, and partners are warmed up to the engineer or surveyor before an important project begins through the LinkedIn profile.

LinkedIn Company Page

Companies and organizations benefit greatly by having their own company page on LinkedIn. There is no charge from LinkedIn to use this basic capability, but you may want to hire a professional to correctly set the page up for your business or organization.

The benefits of a LinkedIn company page are so many that they are best categorized as branding, followership and thought leadership, recruiting and advertising, and management and analysis.

Free Branding Advantages

- gain a LinkedIn web page for your company with logo, banner, specialties, and SEO-capable description
- gain increased presence on Google search, LinkedIn search, status updates, and from employee profiles
- gain the ability to highlight separate brands or divisions with a "showcase page"
- have your company logo appear on your employee's individual LinkedIn profiles (if set up properly)
- gain the ability to post and share content, engaging with clients, partners, and prospects

Free Followership and Thought Leadership Benefits

- gain company followers who will receive your company's status updates in their personal news feeds
- post company and industry news and articles to all followers, sharing valuable content and news
- segment your content to different audiences, sending targeted posts to subsets of your followers or from showcase page updates

Recruiting and Advertising (Free and Premium Benefits)

- advertise your company or services to targeted individuals through LinkedIn
- post jobs that link to your company page.
- create a career page linked to your company page
- drive candidate interest in your company (According to LinkedIn, candidates who are followers of your company page are more likely to want to work at your company.)

Management and Analysis

- use multiple page administrators to manage your company page
- analyze the popularity of your posts with LinkedIn's built in analytics features
- review demographics of your page followers
- see followers in company page analytics:

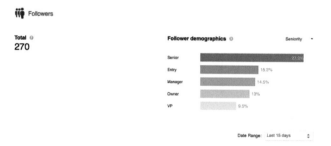

- see page views and unique visitors using the company page analytics:

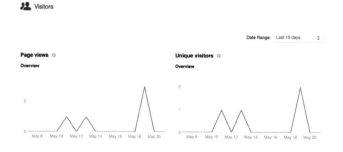

LinkedIn Fun Fact: As of this writing (2016) there are more than four million business pages on LinkedIn.

Requirements for a LinkedIn Company Page

LinkedIn Company pages are established online by individual users. The starting point is a properly set up LinkedIn individual profile that has either an intermediate or all-star profile strength and several connections. This makes sense. LinkedIn wants legitimate users to be able to create the free LinkedIn company page.

Other requirements include the following:

The person setting up the page (admin) must have the position and company listed in the Experience section of his profile and a confirmed e-mail address from the company.

The company's e-mail domain must be unique for that organization.

Do not use Gmail or Yahoo or other generic e-mail addresses for this company page project.

Content to Post on Your Company Page

What your company posts online for LinkedIn, Facebook, Twitter, or Instagram has a major impact on your company brand. If your employees are engaging with the content, it also impacts their individual personal brands. Here is a list of possible content to post on a company page:

- blog articles from company website—with a link
- thought leadership content
- tips and ideas
- industry news and articles
- employee updates
- company news and updates
- upcoming events
- partner or affiliate news
- community initiatives
- customer photo and thank-you

TIP: Try to keep at least 80 percent of your content informational and helpful. Less than 20 percent should be directly about your product or service.

Here is a sample post (below) from Post Road Consulting's LinkedIn company page. Notice the analytics for the post, which is only viewable by page administrators.

Recent Updates

Post Road Consulting LLC This is back in the news: Time to change your password.

 A hacker is reportedly selling the stolen emails and passwords of 117 million LinkedIn users

businessinsider.com · A hacker known as "Peace" is selling what is reportedly account information from 117 million LinkedIn users — including email addresses and passwords.

Like · Comment · Share · 3 days ago

LinkedIn Fun Fact: There is a 50 percent increase in comments when a LinkedIn page post contains a question.

There is a 98 percent increase in comments when a LinkedIn page post contains an image.

Get More Company Page Followers

- Ask employees to link profile in their Experience section to the company page.
- Add link or plug-in to company website that points to the LinkedIn company page.
- Add link or badge to the company page on your e-mail signature—with request to follow.
- Promote the page on Facebook, Twitter, or Google +.
- Ask your first-level connections to follow via an InMail note (start by following their page).
- Add invitation to follow and link at bottom of your blog posts.
- Add invitation to follow on all written documents.
- Ask partners to follow (start by following their pages).
- Ask customers to follow (start by following their pages).
- Use images on posts and ask questions for better engagement.

Finding and Following Other Company Pages

Find company pages by entering the name in the search bar and selecting the drop-down titled "Companies." You can also click on the logo of the page from the status updates in your news feed or directly from employee profile pages.

Consider following the company pages of your partners, vendors, and clients. These pages will show up on your personal LinkedIn profile under Companies at the bottom.

If you are a job seeker, be sure to follow the company pages of the organizations you are interested in working at. The recruiter will be more interested in candidates that are company page followers. Also look for the Career Page section or any posted jobs.

Salespeople can also learn valuable intelligence from a LinkedIn company page. Be the first one to hear about a major event at your client or prospect's business. Then be the first one to InMail your prospect with a personal targeted approach.

Now that we have covered the company aspects of your personal brand, it's time to turn to LinkedIn Groups.

Resources for Chapter 12

Register at the companion website (http://www.linkedinforpersonalbranding .com) for information on the following:

- company page requirements
- how to add a company Page
- how to edit a company page
- how to add a company logo to an employee profile (employees associated with a company page)
- how to send a targeted update
- LinkedIn mention feature

CHAPTER 13

LinkedIn Groups and Your Personal Brand

You may be asking: How is my personal brand related to my LinkedIn Groups? That's a fair question, but I believe that everything you do online is tied to your personal brand. Here are five ways that the groups and your brand will intersect:

1. **Users will find your profile in a LinkedIn Group.** They will associate you as a member, especially if you are an active participant. You will likely be engaging with people and content within a group conversation.
2. **You might decide to start your own LinkedIn Group.** In this scenario, you are the group owner and establish the group rules.
3. **Group membership makes your profile more readily found in a LinkedIn Advanced People Search.**
4. **Jobs are posted within LinkedIn Groups.** Group members who post jobs are targeting the group members as likely candidates.
5. **Your LinkedIn Group badges may be displayed on your profile.** These will reflect your professional interests and affiliations.

Let's start with some basics about LinkedIn Groups.

Group Classifications

LinkedIn Groups are now classified as either "standard" or "unlisted." Standard groups are searchable. Both managers and members can invite or approve membership in standard groups. Unlisted groups are not searchable and membership is only available through manager invitation. Subgroups are no longer supported or available. Understanding the group classifications upfront is important so you understand how to find and select the right groups for you.

Group Posting and Sharing

As of the end of 2015, there were many changes for group members regarding posting and sharing of content. Discussions are now called conversations. Your conversations and comments will be private within the group.

As a member, you can now post instantly to the group. No more waiting for the manager to approve. If your posts are questionable (from the perspective of the LinkedIn filters), they will be put in a moderation queue for the group managers to assess. LinkedIn does an initial filter of content and then the group managers can still move your post if it's inappropriate.

LinkedIn Group members now have the ability to add images and @mentions to enhance posts and conversations. Your posting and comments will be noticed within your LinkedIn Group and reflect on your brand.

Jobs Tab in Groups

Each LinkedIn Group has a Jobs tab. If you are a job seeker, consider checking this tab regularly because the posts are only live here for two weeks.

Be More Strategic with Groups

While you are focusing on your personal brand with LinkedIn, this is a perfect time to reassess where you stand with your LinkedIn Groups. Here are five ways to approach your groups now:

1. **Strategize.** Today is the perfect day to update your goals in relation to your groups. Ask yourself how you can provide value to the group and not just what the group can do for you and your business. What are your personal goals related to LinkedIn Groups? Many group members want to be known as thought leaders or helpful contributors. Others focus on gathering intelligence or networking. You may have different goals relating to each of your priority groups.

2. **Assess your groups.** Determine which groups are the priority for your business, career, and personal brand. You may join up to one hundred groups. Be selective and pick the best groups! Evaluate the following: goals, rules, manager, membership, and conversations. Delete the low-value groups now and focus your precious time only on the ones that are most relevant to your success.

3. **Network.** LinkedIn Groups are often a great place to network. In addition to sending a personalized InMail or being helpful with content, try some of the new features to engage your network. You can @mention someone within a group conversation. You can also invite him or her into a standard group or approve his or her membership. Consider the nice touch of that online invitation after you just met a valuable new contact!

4. **Post and share great content.** The content you share in your groups needs to be aligned with the mission of each group and be a great reflection of your personal brand. If you stay away from promotional or spammy content and focus on providing value to your group, your posts and comments will be welcome. Now you can add images to your content for greater emphasis and engagement. (See chapter 15 about sharing content.)

5. **Stay up to date and manage your time.** There are new ways to stay up to date easily with your groups. Download the mobile app for LinkedIn Groups. Take a quick daily scan of your group activity using the Group Highlights feature or the e-mail digest.

TIP: Read and follow "group rules" before posting any content or commenting.

Always focus on posting helpful and relevant content. Try doing this consistently. You will gain followers and hopefully new career and sales opportunities as a result.

Ten Types of LinkedIn Groups to Consider Joining

1. **Your university alumni groups.** These may be university managed or independent of your school. Some larger universities have dozens of groups to choose from, sometimes broken out by department, fraternities, and so on.

2. **Your company groups.** Definitely join the groups your company is sponsoring or managing. For many companies, this is a key customer focus strategy. If you aren't ready to engage, use this group to listen and learn.

3. **Your organizations.** The organizations you belong to probably have LinkedIn Groups and Facebook pages. This allows you to stay connected in between your monthly meetings.

4. **Your industry groups.** There are thousands of industry groups on LinkedIn. Join them to learn, network, and engage.

5. **Functional groups.** Find a group with similar technical expertise, such as operations, finance, sales, or marketing. Dig deeper to find more specific functional groups: digital marketing, CFO, and so on.

6. **Community- or geographic-based groups.** Search for these niche groups that might be valuable for you.

7. **Customer groups.** Consider where your customers spend their time online. Find your target market in LinkedIn Groups.

8. **Career and job search groups.** It's no surprise that LinkedIn has many career, job search, and talent-related groups. You can find pretty much anything within these categories.

9. **Vendor groups.** You may be invited to a group managed by your vendor. Join it! This may even be an unlisted private group that supports the work you do together.

10. **Company alumni groups:** These may be company sponsored or managed by an ex-employee. Big companies always have networks like this, and they are very valuable.

Google+ and Facebook also have very active groups that you may want to consider. Depending on your needs, they may be even better than a LinkedIn Group for you.

Evaluate Your Group Options

Now that you have found Groups to join, it's time to prioritize the groups as they relate to your brand, goals, and network.

Group Evaluation Factors

Number of members	Make sure it's big enough.
Name and description of group	Is this in sync with your brand?
Group owners and managers	Who are they exactly? Are they people you wish to know?
Quality of members	Who belongs to this group? What professions do they represent?
Quality of conversations and engagement	Are the conversations helpful and informative?
Group rules	What are the rules? It's much better to be in a group with rules.

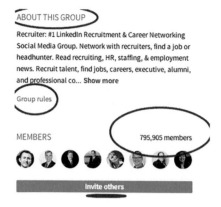

Display Your Group Badges

You can manage the display of your group badges. LinkedIn allows the user to display or hide the group badges from an individual profile. Showing your group badges is normally a good idea but not always. If you are in a passive job search, you may want to hide a job seeker group badge. Or you may want to narrow or adjust the focus by managing the badge visibility on your profile.

Posting Content to Groups

Be especially careful of any content posted in a LinkedIn Group. Look for the group rules and follow them! Veering from the rules may put you into a more restricted status with all LinkedIn Groups and managers.

This is generally good advice for any group: Don't post advertisements or information about your product or service. Don't post links unless the group allows it. Many groups with an overload of links and ads become very spammy. Instead, post helpful thought leadership questions and comments.

TIP: Always find and follow LinkedIn Group rules.

LinkedIn Groups can help you be found on a search, land a job or candidate, be noticed for your expertise, and build a network. LinkedIn Groups are part of the thought leadership opportunities available on LinkedIn.

"LinkedIn Group Membership is a privilege and a responsibility. It is not a place to promote yourself or your business. Be helpful and use LinkedIn Groups to build valuable relationships."

Felix Giannini, CEO of Lexco Inc.

TIP: Read about Felix's success with LinkedIn Publishing and Groups in chapter 16.

Resources for Chapter 13

Register at the companion website (http://www.linkedinforpersonalbranding .com) for information on the following:

- LinkedIn Groups listing
- how to find and join groups
- general limits and information for groups
- editing group information and group settings
- groups: getting started
- how to delete a comment in a LinkedIn Group

Thought Leadership

CHAPTER 14

Thought Leader: Content and Positioning

Business leaders today are establishing their own personal brands with thought leadership. There is also a growing energy around "influencer marketing," "brand ambassadors," and "employee advocacy," which are fueled by content and thought leadership. This is happening across all industries, functions, and levels. It is very likely that both you and your company are striving to be considered as thought leaders.

According to Wikipedia, "A **thought leader** can refer to an individual or firm that is recognized as an authority in a specialized field and whose expertise is sought and often rewarded."

Carefully consider your scope of expertise because if your topic is too broad or if you have multiple areas of expertise, your thought leader brand may get lost. You may want to focus on a niche or microspecialty.

> "38% of LinkedIn users are not engaging in thought leadership activities but hope to in the future."
>
> **Survey by Post Road Consulting LLC, June 2016**

Keeping your expertise to yourself will not help your brand or anyone in your network. You may be a true thought leader, but if you aren't sharing your ideas, very few people will know. Become known as a thought leader by doing the following:

- speaking
- writing
- teaching
- advocating
- mentoring
- solving problems
- sharing ideas
- joining communities

- helping others
- leading initiatives

Sharing content with insights is a popular path for most thought leaders. Putting yourself out there as a speaker, writer, or sharer does place you as an expert; however, in the process, you become a continuous learner as well. It puts you in the position of reading, sharing, and contributing with others in your niche. You will be learning and asking questions every step of the way too.

Thought leadership and personal branding is demonstrated throughout an entire LinkedIn profile—whether it's yours or your team's. The publications, patents, certifications, organizations, experience, and summary all play an important part. But now more and more executives and companies are expanding their thought leadership reach with LinkedIn by being more active and electing to

- write or share content as a company or individual,
- produce or share presentations and videos,
- engage with content and industry influencers online,
- engage personally with prospects and customers online, and
- train employees to share and produce valuable content.

There are many ways to use LinkedIn to show and share your expertise. My best advice is to be careful not to use it to blatantly promote yourself or your company. Be helpful and insightful with any comments. Prospects and referral partners will find you organically and from word of mouth if you are sharing expertise and being helpful.

Inventory Your Content for Profiles and Sharing

Start by creating an inventory of your content. What are you currently producing or have available as a personal or company asset now?

First, consider **your own content:**

- blog posts on company or personal website
- personal or company videos
- professional presentations
- company or executive white papers
- company-produced bulletins, articles, books, and so on.
- customer or industry testimonials or case studies
- personal articles or books

Finding your own or company content should be relatively easy. Look on your website and across all your social media channels. Look at your company's marketing, media, image, or brand library. Ask around.

Media Content

Next, take the time to evaluate what online content exists about you or your company or are related to your industry, such as the following:

- television or radio interviews of you
- blogs on third-party websites
- print or online interviews
- video or audio recordings of your speech
- mainstream media articles about your topic or industry

Example 1

My friend Lisa Bonner displays the YouTube video of her TEDx speech on her LinkedIn profile. Many speakers and executives will find online recordings of their speeches.

Example 2

Many companies share YouTube or SlideShare content on a LinkedIn company page. Employees can then add these to their individual profiles.

Example 3

Display third-party-produced video on a LinkedIn profile.

My client and new friend Marie Patel found dozens of terrific YouTube videos across many channels that illustrated her employer's projects.

Marie works for Redniss & Mead, a civil engineering firm. Due to Marie's work, all the engineers and surveyors were able to link the various YouTube videos to their profiles. They found videos of their projects online and shared on LinkedIn. Below is the Experience section of Jorge Periera, principal and senior surveyor, with YouTube videos added as his "professional portfolio."

 Experience

Senior Surveyor
Redniss & Mead, Inc.
June 1995 – Present (20 years 8 months) l Stamford, CT

REDNISS
& MEAD

I serve as a Senior Surveyor and Project Manager on many site development projects. I am responsible for scheduling and coordinating all field work for the firm and works closely with the field crew members on most projects. I am responsible for numerous boundary and topographic surveys, construction layout of projects, client contact and coordination with other team members. I am also responsible for responding to requests for new work with written proposals.

Redniss & Mead, Inc. is a full service consulting and design firm specializing in Civil Engineering, Land Surveying and Land-Use Planning. Located in Stamford, CT, the company has established itself as a leading land-use consultant in the region providing services from project inception to the design and permit phase and through completion to construction.

Stamford Harbor Point   Summer House Beam Raising

Two videos

Industry or Partner Content

Now look at your customers, partners, and industry connections for valuable content.

- "how-to" or product videos or articles from your vendor partner for products or services that you resell
- customer or industry testimonials
- strategic industry articles
- articles, videos, or presentations from your industry association
- articles from LinkedIn's PULSE or other news sites (See the next chapter for more about PULSE.)

Partner/Producer Example

One of my customers is a local insurance company president. Peter's company is a producer for many of the top insurance providers. We used his company's professionally produced "how-to" and "why insurance?" type of videos on YouTube throughout Peter's personal profile. He is also able to share those on a periodic basis as a status update. There is no need for Peter to produce expensive videos when he can leverage his partners' marketing budget.

Evaluate Your Content and Gaps

Now that you have a good inventory and a plan on how you wish to distinguish yourself, it's time to evaluate how that content is in sync with your brand and thought leadership objectives. Select the best samples for your LinkedIn Profile. Some of the content may be better suited for "status updates" or repurposing as a longer blog post. If your company provides continuous status updates to share, you are fortunate. "Employee Advocacy" is an easy way for company employees to become brand ambassadors.

Create Content Goals

Decide what content gaps you have and how you wish to fill them. Will you start writing your own blogs? Or will you share content from influencers or industry partners? Will you create or share videos or presentations? Will you look deeper at your partners and industry for content? How can you help your personal and company brand with content in the future?

I recommend that you read the next three chapters and then come back to answer these pertinent questions.

Thought Leader Positioning

Distinguish yourself as a thought leader by sharing unique insights and being a cutting edge thinker on your topic. Our entire economy is moving toward commoditization. Your business prospects, customers, hiring managers, recruiters, and candidates—all the people we wish to attract— will be drawn to you if you have a special or unique point of view related to your area of expertise.

TIP: Create your unique perspective and share it along with valuable content. Become the "helpful expert."

Here's how I think about this for myself. There are several excellent LinkedIn experts around the globe. Many of them are experts on navigation, search, recruiting, or other aspects.

My thought leadership perspective is focused on building authentic relationships and a personal brand. I speak and write about building a valuable network from face-to-face relationships and being able to seamlessly move from live to online. I want my readers and listeners to think differently about how they use LinkedIn. I focus primarily on quality and helpfulness for sales and recruiting. That's my niche. What is yours?

Let's start with the easiest method of all, which is sharing content from other people. You don't need to be a writer in order to provide valuable content and build your thought leadership brand!

Resources for Chapter 14

Register at the companion website (http://www.linkedinforpersonalbranding .com) for information on the following:

- how to add rich media to your profile
- LinkedIn PULSE

CHAPTER 15

Thought Leader: Share Content on LinkedIn

You definitely want to share content produced or written by yourself and others. Even if you are a prolific writer or daily blogger, it is just good form to share other people's content. Sharing and commenting is a pathway to forging many new relationships. It's a wonderful way to share valuable ideas and add your insightful commentary.

There is no perfect formula for sharing content. There are many different approaches that will work well. If you are thoughtful and helpful and mindful of your network and the LinkedIn platform, you will do very well by sharing content. Don't be afraid—your network will appreciate your shares.

Share Content from within LinkedIn

There is a lot of relevant interesting content throughout LinkedIn that you can like, share, or make compelling comments about. Here's where to look:

> **Your home feed:** Click on Home on the upper-left corner of your profile and scroll down the page to see your personalized home page. You will see the news, updates, and articles connected to your network, your groups, and the companies you are following.
>
> Like or share an article, and many of your first-level connections will view this as your shared post.
>
> **Your groups:** Find your groups under the Interests tab. Within your groups you are likely to find articles and commentary shared by members. You may respond to a posted article or comment with a like or comment, or you may start a new discussion.
>
> Your posts within LinkedIn Groups are now visible to only those group members. Make sure new articles, posts, or

comments that you put in LinkedIn Groups are appropriate and follow the group's community rules.

PULSE: Find content by media source, influencer, or category channel under LinkedIn's PULSE. Your likes, comments, and shares will be visible to your network and beyond. Look for and click on the forward arrow in the PULSE article to share.

Elevate: Share content from LinkedIn's Elevate app if your company is participating. Shares will appear similar to your other status update shares on the LinkedIn home feed.

Share Content from Your Inventory

When considering your personal brand and thought leadership strategy, think about the following:

What to share. Make sure your shared content is in sync with your niche or market. Remember to keep your content helpful and not product focused.

How often to share. Don't oversaturate your connections with your own content, but you want to be visible. Decide how often to share and create a plan based on that. Be mindful of the right amount of sharing for your network.

Where to share. Share on your home feed, status updates, or in a LinkedIn Group. For groups, be sure to make the content directly relevant. Always follow the group rules that are posted within each group.

How to share. Simply copy the URL of your website blog post or YouTube channel video and paste into your home feed or group feed as a "status update." Your company blog may have social sharing buttons you can use, which is even easier. Wait for the image to populate. Add your insightful comment or idea. Check your post after it's been shared to make sure it looks great. You can delete a post if there is a problem.

Whether to automate. You may decide to automate your shared posts. I prefer to post each one manually, but I know others who prefer automation. If you automate, I still urge you to check daily for quality!

Sharing Directly from Third-Party Sites

Magazine Articles or Blog Posts from Third Parties: Easily share content from most major blog or media sites by using the share buttons. Share buttons are commonly on the side or bottom of an article. Click the LinkedIn logo to share directly to LinkedIn. All major sites have these all set up for easy sharing.

Most of the built in share buttons direct the share to your personal status update or home feed. Some also allow you to share to a company page. Copy the URL of the article if you wish to share it in a LinkedIn Group. (Make sure the group rules allow your topic.)

Step-by-Step Sharing: Forbes Example

Step 1: Find the Share buttons

Step 2: Select LinkedIn as shown here, and then Forbes will create a post for LinkedIn as shown below:

Share a YouTube Video: Instantly share a relevant industry video directly from YouTube to LinkedIn with the built in share buttons from YouTube.

First click Share.

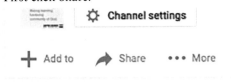

Then choose the LinkedIn icon.

Finally, you will see that YouTube has created a post that you may now share on LinkedIn.

Share a SlideShare Presentation: Instantly share a presentation from SlideShare to LinkedIn with the built in share buttons. Simply click on the logo icons for the appropriate social media platform to get the post started.

Share Content with a Mention: Congratulate your best connections and industry leaders with an @mention on LinkedIn. You are sharing content and also recognizing another leader. Simply use @ and type in the person's name to show the drop-down selection. This @mention becomes a hyperlink and notification. Your connection will be thrilled with the @mention!

Use the LinkedIn Sharing Bookmarklet

TIP: Install the bookmarklet onto your browser bar for easy sharing.

LinkedIn Fun Fact: The best time to post on LinkedIn for engagements is 10 a.m. to 11 a.m. EST.

A Note Especially for Company Employees

Are you an employee of a company? If so, be sure to find and follow your company's social media policies. This is important for everyone but particularly critical if you are working in a regulated industry. Understand your corporate guidelines so you can navigate social media appropriately as it relates to your employer, industry, and clients. On LinkedIn, remember that you are representing both yourself and your company.

Many companies are going beyond just providing rules or guidelines. Corporate marketing teams are using "employee advocacy" program to distribute preapproved articles for employees. Marketing teams are regularly posting great content with social media share buttons for the employees to like, comment, or share. Think about it—employees should be a company's best brand ambassadors! The smartest marketing teams know how to team up with sales, HR, and other employee groups.

LinkedIn has a new app to make employee sharing easy. It's called "Elevate." Check with your company's marketing pros to see if your company is leveraging this app.

Even without any policy, guideline, app, or marketing content, you should be very safe to like or share content that your company puts on its LinkedIn company page. Easy! Go to your employer's page every week and like, comment, or share an article that you think would be of interest to your network.

As an employee, you may also find good content to share on your company website. The web page is likely to have a social sharing button, too, to make it very simple. Click on the LinkedIn icon to share. If there are no built-in sharing options, simply copy the URL of the webpage and paste it into your LinkedIn status update. Wait for the image to populate and then share.

Check out your company's Twitter, Pinterest, SlideShare, Google+, Instagram, YouTube channel, and all other social media platforms. The easiest way to locate your company's social sites is to look for the links on the company website.

Since the website and social media content is already posted online by your marketing team, it's a pretty safe bet the team would like you to share it. After that, consider industry content produced in LinkedIn PULSE or in trade magazines. Find out if you can share content or whether it needs prior approval from your manager.

TIP: Always follow the social media policy from your company!

A Note Especially for Company Executives

Your employee's online profiles and activity should be the most power-ful and effective way to share the excitement about your company brand. This professional online energy will impact sales, recruiting, and all of your department's efforts. Every LinkedIn profile of your employees mat-ters. They're your best ambassadors.

Make sure that your sales and recruiting professionals know the proper etiquette and methodology of finding and engaging with new prospects, candidates, longtime customers, and content. You may be surprised how many of your team really understand how to leverage LinkedIn properly for business.

Without training, policies, and guidelines, social media for your employees is like the Wild West. Your employees will be online doing whatever they feel like doing. Don't assume they know how to leverage the opportunities on LinkedIn, even factoring in their age bracket. It's your job to set policies and guidelines and to create goals. All of this also requires training for your team.

As a corporate leader, don't miss out on the most exciting trend called "employee advocacy." This is the ultimate social media leverage for a company or organization. It starts with great content posted on LinkedIn and other social media channels by your marketing team. Your team becomes brand ambassadors for your business.

TIP: Create brand ambassadors and thought leaders at your company.

Company employees are then trained to engage, like, share, and com-ment. Imagine the amplification of your brand messaging when your employees are sharing the posts with their personal connections and net-work. All of that sharing will generate more profile views, which is why your company effort needs to start there.

Invest in your team with LinkedIn profile, networking, and etiquette training, whether you do a formal employee advocacy program or not. At a bare minimum, you want the team to look impressive, share content, and be able to properly respond when clients or prospects find them on LinkedIn.

Step one	Institute **brand ambassador program.** Oversee personal branding of your team. Incorporate company marketing assets. Train employees on branding, basic navigation, and networking.
Step two	Institute **employee advocacy program.** Create content and advocacy program. Train and remind employees.

Step three	Consider training your sales or HR teams on the advance techniques of **social selling** or **social recruiting**.

As a corporate leader, consider your role as a thought leader. One great way to expand your impact is by using the LinkedIn Publisher platform, which is discussed in the very next chapter.

Resources for Chapter 15

Register at the companion website (http://www.linkedinforpersonalbranding .com) for information on the following:

- how to share an update on LinkedIn
- how to add the LinkedIn Sharing Bookmarklet to your browser bar
- LinkedIn @mentions
- LinkedIn Elevate
- LinkedIn PULSE
- how to show or hide activity updates about yourself
- visibility of updates you share on LinkedIn

CHAPTER 16

Thought Leader: Blogging with LinkedIn Publisher

My client and friend Felix Giannini is a thought leader on the LinkedIn platform. He owns and manages a security and life safety systems business called Lexco Inc. (www.lexcosecurity.com). He doesn't post articles about buying or using alarm systems. Instead, his topics include quality, personal security, corporate security, and business continuity information. He is an expert in many aspects of security and life safety. Felix is an industry thought leader, speaker, and expert witness.

Felix has been using LinkedIn successfully as a thought leader. He has gained many prominent new customers and built relationships with other leaders in the security industry.

Felix has primarily focused his thought leadership efforts on the LinkedIn Publishing platform and LinkedIn Groups. Let's discuss the benefits of posting blogs on LinkedIn and then we'll circle back shortly to review Felix's publishing results for 2015.

Benefits of Posting Blogs on LinkedIn Publisher Platform

Blogging on LinkedIn offers everyone the chance to become a writer. If you are a subject matter expert, then why not show your thought leadership by blogging.

Ten Benefits of Blogging on LinkedIn

1. **Expand your brand.** Posting on LinkedIn builds your personal brand as a thought leader. The topics you select are a direct tie to you and your work.
2. **Expand your visibility in your network.** Your LinkedIn connections receive a notification that you have posted an article. Wow! You don't have to wait for them to arrive at your website or blog page. As your friends and colleagues like and comment on your article, your wider second- and third-level connection network will be exposed to you and your articles.
3. **Expand your visibility beyond your network.** Should your article be selected by LinkedIn PULSE editors, it will be circulated to the larger LinkedIn global audience for even more viewership. Your articles are also visible to many second- and third-level connections as your first-level connections comment and share your post.
4. **Be found through a Google search.** LinkedIn blog posts are perfect for search engines.
5. **Blog (the price is right).** The publishing platform is completely free with a LinkedIn profile. You will not need to invest in a new website in order to start blogging.
6. **Leverage images, hyperlinks, and the opportunity to embed video and slides.** Dress up your post with images. In addition to the header image, add images throughout your post. Link to other articles or sites or embed a video or presentation.
7. **Add credibility and views to your profile.** The posts you write will be displayed on your profile in a prominent position near the top. Your profile views will increase every time you post a blog article.
8. **Use analytics and engagement.** LinkedIn will show you likes, comments, and shares. Use this information to improve and fine tune your posts.
9. **Engage with old and new connections.** You may decide to follow up with people who comment or like your post. I suggest that you thank everyone. You may also receive InMails from your readers. As a result of publishing, expect to receive new invitations, connections, and followers.

10. **Gain customers or be hired.** Yes, this does happen. So now it's time to tell you more about my friend Felix Giannini and how he leverages LinkedIn Publishing.

The LinkedIn Publisher platform is a major improvement and investment made by LinkedIn for the benefit of all users. Even if you are not quite ready to start blogging, you should be receiving notifications about articles written by your friends and colleagues in your LinkedIn inbox. Consider responding to, liking, and commenting on the articles written by your network associates.

Here's an in-depth look at Felix Giannini's success. Felix's company, Lexco Inc., sells security and life safety systems. Felix is a thought leader who leverages LinkedIn Publishing and Groups.

A sampling of Felix's 2015 LinkedIn Publisher blog titles is below:

- "Come Hell and High Water"
- "Be Prepared"
- "Protecting Your Family at Home—Honestly"
- "Protecting Our Houses of Worship"
- "Safety Tips for Seniors"
- "Protecting Your Family from Carbon Monoxide"
- "False Alarms Are Killing Us"

Felix Giannini's publishing results for 2015—wow!

Authored forty two posts, many with more than three hundred views

Shared many posts with his sixty-six LinkedIn Groups (ten-plus million members)

Ranked #1 in the "Professional Like Me" category of Who's Viewed Your Profile rankings

Closed twenty new security system sales

Received more than fifty unsolicited recruiter inquires (he is not in a formal job search)

Received thousands of endorsements

Received regular positive feedback from community

Built many new significant industry relationships

Gained 4,400 followers, many of whom are not connections but like to read his posts

Ten Tips on How to Use LinkedIn Publisher for Blogging

The LinkedIn blogging platform is very easy to use and navigate. You will find it on your LinkedIn home page on the right hand side of the main feed. Look for "Write a Post." Click there to get into your own publisher dashboard.

Here are ten tips on making the most of the LinkedIn Publisher platform:

1. **Make sure you are actually writing a blog post.** Sometimes LinkedIn users will publish an advertisement, announcement, or just a link to another site. The best way to use LinkedIn Publisher is to post a valuable article. Pick a great thought leadership topic for your brand. (See examples below.)

2. **Longer posts are preferred on LinkedIn.** The minimum length should be 500 words, but always shoot for 1,500 to 3,000 words if possible. Many reputable studies have suggested that the longer posts are shared more often.

3. **Select the right headline for your post.** Here are three great reasons: Your connections will get your article headline in their inbox, so you want to make it enticing to read and like. Your headline and image is viewable on your LinkedIn personal profile. And finally, your headline is searchable by Google.

4. **Incorporate great images.** Add a header image that really pops and ties into your blog post. Also consider adding images within the post.

5. **Add hyperlinks to other related content or websites.**

6. **Consider embedding or linking to a video or presentation if it is in sync with your article.** I usually make a corresponding SlideShare presentation for most of my blog posts. I link over from the LinkedIn Publisher platform to SlideShare or YouTube.

7. **End your article with a call to action of some kind.** Ask a question or ask for comments to your post. Ask for followers or a connection or a review of your website.

8. **Share your post outside of LinkedIn.** Share on Facebook, Twitter, Google+, Pinterest, and all of your social media channels. Within LinkedIn, consider which groups to share the article with, being mindful of group rules and culture.

9. **Respond to comments and likes.** Send a thank you InMail to your connections for likes and shares. Publicly thank the people who comment.

10. **Analyze your blog results with the built-in analytics features.** Analyze page views, likes, comments, shares, dates, and demographics. Use the analytics as well as the comments

and feedback to refine your article or future articles. You may edit a LinkedIn post at any time.

Publishing on LinkedIn can be professionally rewarding and gratifying! Why not start today?

Resources for Chapter 16

Chapter 18: Rate Yourself

Register at the companion website (http://www.linkedinforpersonalbranding .com) for information on the following:

- long-form posts on LinkedIn, an overview (publisher)
- more writing tips for LinkedIn Publisher
- how to edit a LinkedIn Publisher post
- blog topic idea list—download

CHAPTER 17

Thought Leader: SlideShare and Video

Presentations and video are both wonderfully visual ways to enhance your brand message. My absolute favorite presentation platform is SlideShare. Individuals and companies can create a SlideShare account for free.

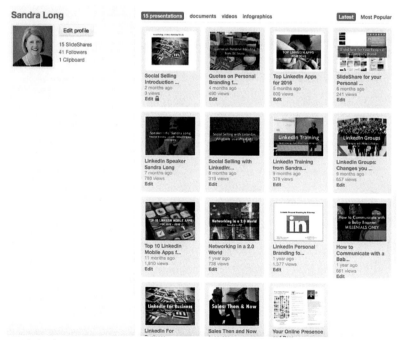

SlideShare is one of the top one hundred most visited websites globally. Users upload and share presentations, documents, videos, and infographics. SlideShare was recently acquired by LinkedIn and is now integrated within your LinkedIn account.

**Seventeen Reasons SlideShare Is Great for
Personal and Company Branding**

1. **Search Engine Optimization, or SEO.** SlideShare helps you be found through Google. The presentation title becomes the URL. Use SEO-friendly descriptions and tags for greater visibility.

2. **Be found within the LinkedIn environment.** Now that Slide-Share is becoming more integrated, we are seeing more entry points from LinkedIn directly to SlideShare.

3. **Reach new audiences within SlideShare community.** With seventy million monthly visitors (as of this writing), your presentation can be easily found here. You and your work can be discovered through a specific SlideShare search or as a result of your presentation being selected as a featured presentation. Your presentation may also be added to the "featured topic" section or listed as trending in a particular social media channel.

4. **Easy social sharing.** Your followers and connections can easily like, download, embed, or clip your slides with SlideShare social sharing buttons.

5. **Be more visual.** Expand the appeal of your message and thought leadership by presenting your topic in multiple ways, such as through presentation and video formats.

6. **Free (the price is right).** Create an account and share presentations using the free SlideShare account.

7. **Enhance your LinkedIn profile with SlideShare presentations.** Your viewers will get a better understanding of your thought leadership capabilities.

8. **Build a community of followers and online friends.** Users may get followers and likes for their presentations, all of which can lead to learning and new relationships.

9. **Share your ideas online.** Are you a speaker? Share your presentations with your audience online so your audience can easily consume your content and follow you.

10. **Analyze how your presentations are doing with SlideShare analytics.** See likes, comments, and downloads. Fine-tune based on the feedback and results.

11. **Link to other sites or valuable content from within your slide deck.**

12. **Improve your website.** Embed your SlideShare decks directly into your website. You can easily find the embed code for each presentation.

13. **Continue learning and connecting.** Research your industry and find influencers. Learn from others by connecting, liking, and reviewing other people's great content.

14. **Enhances sales or recruiting.** Create SlideShare presentations that are helpful in your natural sales or recruiting process. Answer the questions your prospects are asking early on, even before a call, meeting, or interview. Use SlideShare to "presell."

15. **Acquire leads.** SlideShare has an optional lead generation form, which is customizable and is an affordable premium-type feature. Or you can include a call-to-action with clickable links for free.

16. **Mobile-friendly.** SlideShare is completely mobile-friendly for your readers and audiences.

17. **Embed video.** Upload and embed a YouTube video within your presentation for added pizzazz and SEO power.

Author's Example: "Sales Then and Now" is my most popular presentation, with more than thirteen thousand views in less than eighteen months. The first week, it received more than eight thousand views. I embed this presentation on my profile and the Post Road Consulting website.

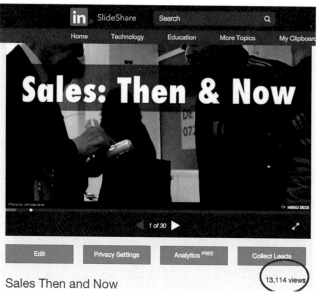

Sales Then and Now

Featured SlideShare Examples: The top SlideShares are displayed as "Featured SlideShares." Or "Trending in Social Media."

Setting up a SlideShare Account

Create your own personal or company SlideShare profile and account. Log in through SlideShare or LinkedIn. I login using my LinkedIn credentials. SlideShare will populate a portion of your profile using LinkedIn data, but you may edit and add descriptions and links.

Take a few minutes to set up your account properly. Go to "Account Settings," then "Profile Details." Here you may edit. Select "Account Type" if you wish to switch from the default to an alternative designation such as company, university, nonprofit, and so on. Add your website and company name and select your industry from the drop-down menu. Like LinkedIn, the SlideShare industry list is fairly limited, so choose the closest one to your occupation or specialty.

Link your account to your website and to your other social media channels by adding in the URLs in the appropriate places.

Creating Presentation Content for SlideShare

Make your content more visual, interesting, and connected. Readers are overwhelmed with content. SlideShare is a fresh new way to get your point across in an easily digestible way.

Tips for Your Presentations
- Use large colorful images and minimize the use of words.
- Select interesting fonts.
- Create a consistent look and feel.
- Add a captivating and SEO-friendly headline.
- Incorporate links to other content after page 4.
- Embed YouTube videos into presentations.
- Optimize for SEO as you upload presentations.

How to Optimize for SEO as You Upload to SlideShare

The SEO optimization starts before you upload. Carefully consider the file name because it automatically becomes the URL. Include the keywords that connect to your personal brand if possible.

As soon as you upload your presentation, you have some immediate work to do on the behalf of your upload.

Select a headline that is compelling and contains keywords. Keep the headline length under fifty-five characters so the full headline is viewable on Google search.

Use keywords and tagging to promote search. Take the time to write a substantial description of the presentation on SlideShare because Google recognizes the first 155 characters for search purposes. Then select the best twenty tags for each presentation. Both the description and tags are perfect places for keywords.

Finish your upload by selecting a category and adjusting the privacy settings. The settings allow you to decide about views and ability to download. Your slide may also be selected for clipping to a reader's clipboard, if you allow that in the settings.

Video for Thought Leadership and Personal Branding

Presentations and videos bring your online brand to life for your connections and network.

YouTube videos are an obvious first choice. Putting YouTube videos on your LinkedIn profile is a very effective way to demonstrate your thought leadership. Both YouTube and Vimeo videos can be directly linked to a LinkedIn profile.

Video Options
- your own videos, created by and starring you
- videos in which you are interviewed or featured
- your company videos
- videos of projects that you participated in
- videos of your partners or products that you represent

The great news is that the YouTube videos you share may not have been created or uploaded by you. Sharing the right video from your company or partner can impact your brand too.

YouTube Fun Fact: YouTube has more than 1.3 billion users!

Where to Post Videos and Presentations on LinkedIn

Upload files for presentation/video or link to YouTube, Vimeo, or SlideShare on your LinkedIn profile

Share links to a YouTube video or SlideShare presentation as a LinkedIn status update

Share a video or presentation link on a group update (be mindful of group rules)

Embed video in a LinkedIn Publisher post

Share links to a video as a company page update

Thought Leadership will differentiate you from your competitors. Decide which thought leadership path is best for you. If you are a content producer, consider expanding into LinkedIn Publishing, SlideShare, and video. Consider the types of content you share as well as where and how you share.

Resources for Chapter 17

Register at the companion website (http://www.linkedinforpersonalbranding .com) for information on the following:

- how to set up a SlideShare account
- How to share your SlideShare content
- SlideShare analytics
- how to connect SlideShare to your social profiles
- SlideShare FAQ

Moving Forward

CHAPTER 18

Rate Yourself

We all like to know where we stand. And why not? There are many ways you can measure your progress using the data-rich LinkedIn platform.

Metrics are available for individuals, groups, and companies. For our purposes, we will focus on LinkedIn metrics for *individuals*, such as the following:

- profile strength
- connections and followers
- profile views and ranking
- publishing post analytics
- social selling index

Profile Strength: Beginner to All-Star?

As soon as you start populating your LinkedIn profile, your ranking will quickly rise to *all-star ranking*. I have seen mediocre profiles that received an all-star ranking. It's the first basic way to measure your profile. You definitely want to be an all-star because it is indicative of the profile completeness. Don't stop at all-star, however. Aim much higher for your profile to be found and fully express your personal brand.

Profile Strength

All-Star

LinkedIn Connections

First-level connections are reserved for our most meaningful relationships on LinkedIn. It requires acceptance from both parties, unlike a "follower" relationship. Second-level connections are our "friends of friends" and typically comprise a great pool of potential introductions and referrals. Third-level connections are the next step removed from second-level. You can identify your relationship level by the icon on the person's profile page when you view from your account.

2nd

One of the most important personal metrics is the number of first-level connections. In my opinion, your first-level connections are to be cherished and protected. For most of us, we want to connect with people we know, like, and trust. Accepting strangers into our network might make sense too if there is good reason that aligns with your networking or branding strategy.

You might decide to connect with people in your industry or from your city that you wish to know. I suggest reviewing every profile carefully before deciding to connect. You are essentially giving away your e-mail address to every new connection, so don't just accept anyone and everyone on LinkedIn.

LinkedIn Fun Fact: The average number of connections for a CEO on LinkedIn is 930.

LinkedIn, 2016

LinkedIn Followers

LinkedIn now allows for "followers." Influencers and people who actively publish on LinkedIn tend to have the most followers. Following is a perfect strategy if you wish to receive posts from an individual but are not yet ready to connect.

If you start publishing blog posts on LinkedIn, you are more likely to get your own unique followers. Your follower number will be equal or larger than your number of connections, as all of your connections are automatically considered followers.

Who's Viewed Your Profile

"Who's Viewed Your Profile" is one of the most popular features on LinkedIn. Your actual visibility will vary depending on your account type and if you allow others to see your profile.

If you are paying for a premium service, your visibility of your specific profile viewers will extend to the last ninety days. Otherwise, you will only be able to see the five most recent viewers within the last ninety days (assuming you are sharing your profile to others). If you check this regularly, it might not be an issue for you. LinkedIn also provides weekly trends graph and additional insights about your viewers in the free version.

The other factor on visibility is the settings on your account and the person who viewed you. You will only be able to see the complete profile of your viewers if their settings are open to this. If the viewer has their profile setting on "private mode," then you will only see "LinkedIn Member." There is also a semiprivate mode that provides partial profile information.

Knowing the number of views over the last ninety days is a good metric to watch and compare over time. LinkedIn also lets you compare your profile viewing rank with other professionals like you (or company) and with your entire network. Check "How You Rank for Profile Views."

LinkedIn Fun Fact: Number of profile views: forty-five million per day.

LinkedIn, 2016

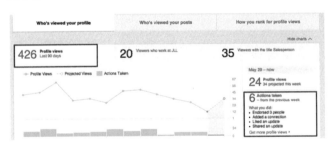

LinkedIn also provides specific suggestions to the user, such as "Easy Ways to Get More Views."

Easy ways to get more views

Join this group
Share your insights and expertise with your colleagues to increase your visibility.

Add this skill

Publishing Analytics for Bloggers

Start to publish posts, and you will be able to attract followers in addition to your regular LinkedIn connections. You'll also learn the demographics of your readers, top locations, job titles, and traffic sources.

For each post, look for the number of views, likes, comments, and shares.

Once you decide to publish blog articles, you will become immediately interested in the analytics. Number of views for each post is the first critical measure.

Social Selling Index (SSI)—It's Not Just for Salespeople!

The social selling index (SSI) measures four attributes: establish a personal brand, find the right people, engage with insights, and build strong relationships. All of these are important for everyone on LinkedIn—salespeople, recruiters, hiring managers, job seekers, entrepreneurs, attorneys, consultants, and senior executives. Don't be scared away by the name "social selling index"!

Each attribute has a top score of twenty-five, and the highest total score is one hundred. This SSI score was originally available for Sales Navigator license holders. Now we all have access to this measurement tool. The average scores tend to be very low so don't be scared away by a low score—because now you can work on raising it higher!

Here is my SSI score: Even though I am active on LinkedIn every day and I use Sales Navigator, I can see that I will improve by "engaging with insights."

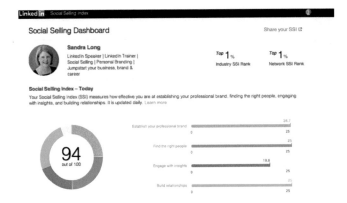

Notice your own score and where you rank within your network, company, or industry. In my industry (professional training and coaching), the average score is sixteen. Within my network, the average score is forty-two. This makes sense to me because I am connected to clients and many like-minded sales, marketing, and talent executives.

The SSI link is available to everyone; please check the companion website for your own score.

TIP: Don't be discouraged by a low score. Most scores are very low. The best idea is to use it as motivation to improve.

Let's dig into each one a bit further. I suspect the algorithms will change over time, so your best bet is to experiment with which actions are impacting your scores. Some of the scoring is based on use of Sales Navigator. The score is updated regularly.

SSI element	Sandra's tips for you
Establish a personal brand	Complete an optimized profile. Publish posts. Generate endorsements. Interact with content.
Find the right people	Use advanced search. For sales navigator users, actively use all the advanced features. Use keyword modifiers and Boolean search. Join groups.
Engage with insights	Post content. Comment and share in groups. Like, share, and comment. Send InMail. Publish content and engage with commenters.
Build the right relationships	Increase connections. Make multiple connections at accounts. Connect internally and leverage TeamLink. Nurture relationships.

This is just the beginning of using metrics on LinkedIn. Here's my list of the top personal metrics to monitor and focus on. Start with your profile and display your fabulous, unique, and authentic personal brand. After your profile is complete, focus on your connections and overall activity.

Sandra's Recommended Goals for Readers

1. **Have an "all-star" profile in combination with a twenty-plus score for the personal branding element of the SSI.** Make sure your profile optimistically and authentically represents your personal brand.
2. **Increase the number of first-level connections. This should increase each week as you meet new people.** Carefully consider each invitation.
3. **Increase the number of profile views.** This will increase as a result of your online activity and offline meetings.
4. **Improve total SSI score.** Find where you need to improve, and focus on that element.
5. **Improve the number of posts and followers.** Think about starting to blog on LinkedIn. Make sure you are posting an actual blog that will generate interest from others. It should never be self-promoting.

You deserve a hearty congratulations for getting this far! We are on to our last chapter!

Resources for Chapter 18

Appendix B, for settings

Register at the companion website (http://www.linkedinforpersonalbranding .com) for information on the following:

- SSI score; what is your score?
- how to view your followers
- LinkedIn connections, an overview
- basic and premium features of "Who's Viewed Your Profile"
- "Who's Viewed Your Profile": trends and insights
- "Who's Viewed Your Profile" FAQ
- analytics for long form posts (LinkedIn Publisher)
- SlideShare analytics

CHAPTER 19

What Now?

Thank you for reading this book about personal branding with LinkedIn. I hope you get the sense that this is a marathon, not a sprint. Thinking about yourself, your role, and the unique value you offer is worth taking some serious time and effort to consider and plan.

I urge you to continue the work of your personal branding. Understand and develop your unique personal and professional gifts. We are living in a time when it is clearly our job to manage our online image. The side benefit is that we will learn and grow from this exercise.

Post Road Consulting recently conducted a survey regarding LinkedIn and personal branding. There are a lot of interesting statistics, including the following:

- 41 percent of respondents spend two to five hours per year updating their profile.
- 28 percent of respondents spend five or more hours per year updating their profile.

I encourage you to spend the time to keep your profile up to date and memorable. Make it a priority for your business and career.

TIP: Start in the beginning with a great LinkedIn profile!

You Can Be Memorable
- tell a story
- be uniquely you
- share a perspective
- be visual
- paint a picture with words
- demonstrate expertise

Engage Professionally on LinkedIn

Be Helpful. Make sure you are engaging online in a helpful way. Try not to self-promote on LinkedIn. Instead, offer your expertise and guidance. Be helpful and not overly sales or product focused. Some of your business will come to you as a result of you being the helpful expert.

Support Your Network. Build relationships by promoting the great accomplishments of your first-level connections.

You may be ready to advance into a more active social selling or social recruiting role. Good for you! Consider upgrading to the LinkedIn premium solutions and learn how to use the tools effectively. Learn to engage with your prospects using the right etiquette and messaging and you will be very successful.

Are You Overwhelmed?

I realize that the advice in this book will be overwhelming for many readers. If that is you, I recommend that you do the following:

1. Focus on your profile and personal brand first. Put the thought leadership out of your head for now, and concentrate on having a **great** profile.
2. Have a 100 percent complete LinkedIn profile.
3. Make sure you have an amazing headshot, headline, and summary.
4. Use the best images and language for your personal brand.
5. Connect with all the people in your professional and personal network.

After you have a genuine and compelling personal brand displayed on your LinkedIn profile, you can return back to read chapters 14 through 18 to enhance your brand with thought leadership activities.

Companion Website

Please refer to appendix A for complete information about the companion website. You will find links relating to all the tips in this book.

Direct Feedback

I am open to your direct feedback. If you have a question, idea, or success story, I may be able to incorporate your thoughts into a future edition. Please e-mail me at sandra@postroadconsulting.com.

Let's Stay Connected

I hope you will decide to stay connected to me after you finish this book. I would like to hear your thoughts, questions, ideas, and suggestions. Also feel free to contact me if you need more help with your team's branding, selling, or recruiting. My e-mail is sandra@postroadconsulting.com.

Please subscribe to my e-mail list at http://www.linkedinforpersonalbranding.com.

Please follow me and Post Road Consulting on social media:

LinkedIn personal page: http://www.linkedin.com/in/longsandra
LinkedIn company page: http://www.linkedin.com/company/post-road-consulting
Facebook page: http://www.facebook.com/sandralongauthor
Twitter: @SandraGLong

Online Reviews—Thank you in advance for helping me!

I will be so grateful for your Amazon and Goodreads reviews. All the readers arrive at this book destination from different perspectives and backgrounds, and I hope that you found nuggets in here to help you with your business or career. I especially liked using the examples of real people in this book, so hopefully that resonated with you too. Thank you in advance for your online reviews!

Here's to Your Success

I truly hope you enjoyed this book and that it has spurred your thinking about yourself. I personally find LinkedIn to be the best current online location for your personal branding. You could take the same principles here and apply some of the strategies and thinking to Facebook, Google, and elsewhere on social media.

Wishing you the ultimate in new business and career success! Please stay in touch!

—Sandra Long

Appendices

APPENDIX A

Reader Resource Section

The companion website is located at http://www.linkedinforpersonal branding.com.

Simply register and subscribe to the Reader Resouce section in the companion website to get additional information related to the book.

Feel free to share the link with your friends and colleagues. I would love to have more readers.

Reader Section

There is a special section of the website especially for my readers. Simply register and subscribe to my e-mail list and you will be able to access the links and downloads. I will not share your e-mail with anyone else.

What is available on the website in the reader section? I have included many valuable links and downloads. Most of these are organized to go along with the book's chapters.

You will find the following:

- more than fifty resources (links and downloads)
- LinkedIn personal branding checklist (download)
- LinkedIn for veterans
- LinkedIn for volunteer and nonprofit boards
- represent yourself accurately and the LinkedIn user agreement
- how to stay "restriction-free" on LinkedIn
- Sandra's list of favorite online tools (download)
- information about a LinkedIn ProFinder profile

If you wish to reach me about the website or the book, please e-mail me at sandra@postroadconsulting.com.

LinkedIn Settings

Managing your settings effectively will impact the perception people have of you and your brand. The settings will also keep your account safer. It's a good idea to have an understanding of the most important LinkedIn settings.

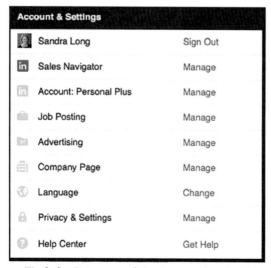

Find the Privacy and Settings under the **Account and Settings** tab for the majority of your personal settings.

At the top of the Settings page, you will find the number of connections, the date you became a LinkedIn member, and the list of any premium accounts.

There are three main categories within the LinkedIn Settings tab.

Section	Examples of functions
Account	Password, e-mail, and data archive
Privacy	Visibility, viewing options, ranking, and blocking
Communications	E-mail, invitations, and group messages

I suggest you evaluate each setting to decide your best option. I have included many (but not all) of the settings with my recommendations.

Sandra's Recommendations on LinkedIn Settings

Name of setting	Where to find	Recommendation from Sandra
E-mail addresses	Account tab under Settings	Always use more than one e-mail address. Select your primary address.
Phone numbers	Account tab under Settings	Add your phone numbers and select primary.
Change password	Account tab under Settings	Change every quarter.
Language	Account tab under Settings	Change as appropriate.
Name, location, and industry	Account tab under Settings or from Edit Profile	Update as appropriate.
Where you're signed in	Account tab under Settings	Check this periodically.
Autoplay videos	Account tab under Settings	Yes.
Showing profile photo	Account tab under Settings	Everyone.
Twitter	Account tab under Settings	Add your Twitter handle so you can post status updates to the public and your Twitter account.
Edit your public profile	Privacy tab under Settings. Find the profile list on the right side.	Allow search engines to find your profile. Make all sections visible to everyone.

Name of setting	Where to find	Recommendation from Sandra
Who can see your connections	Privacy tab under Settings	Keep open to all of your connections. This is a best practice. If you are worried, I suggest you unconnect from anyone that concerns you.
How you rank	Privacy tab under Settings	Select whether you wish to be included in the ranking of profile views.
Viewers of this profile also viewed (displays other people similar to you on the right side of your profile)	Privacy tab under Settings	Turn off if showing your competitors. Turn on if displaying your coworkers.
Sharing profile edits (notify your network about a profile change)	Privacy tab under Settings	Usually you want to keep this on. However, if you are doing a major profile overhaul, it is best to turn it off.
Profile viewing options (people may see that you have viewed their profile)	Privacy tab under Settings	Full profile. Change this as needed. Usually best to show your full profile most of the time.
Notify your connections when you are in the news	Privacy tab under Settings	Yes.
Followers (choose who can follow you and see your updates)	Privacy tab under Settings	Everyone.
Represent your organization on the company page	Privacy tab under Settings	Yes.
Two-step verification	Privacy tab under Settings	Yes.
*** Many additional settings for data privacy, blocking, hiding, and security	Privacy tab under Settings	Review and select if appropriate.
E-mail frequency	Communications tab under Settings	Make your selections.
Who can send you an invitation	Communications tab under Settings	Everyone. Keep it open for anyone to invite you.

Name of setting	Where to find	Recommendation from Sandra
Messages from members	Communications tab under Settings	Select your preferred methods.
Group invitations (receive invitations to join groups)	Communications tab under Settings	Yes.
Group notifications	Communications tab under Settings	Yes.
Group badge on profile	Under Groups, use the "gear" and then the "member settings" button	Keep on for those that you wish to display.
Order of your groups	Under Groups, use the "gear" and then the "Member settings"	Rearrange order of groups on your profile.
Unconnect	Profile or connection tab. The best place to unconnect is from the Connections tab (scroll down)	Unconnect.
Premium badge and open profile	Edit Profile, then Edit PREMIUM. For open profile communications, also go to Communications tab under Settings for "Messages from Members."	Select Premium Profile if you have a premium account and Open Profile if you want everyone on LinkedIn to be able to message you.

Resources for Appendix B

Register at the companion website (http://www.linkedinforpersonalbranding .com) for information on the following:

- managing and changing your account and privacy settings
- managing your account and privacy settings from the mobile app
- changing, adding, or editing e-mail addresses

LinkedIn Specifications and Character Counts

LinkedIn Profile Image Specifications and Character Counts

For images, use PNG, JPG, or GIF file types.

Profile Photo/Headshot

These may be between 200 × 200 and 500 × 500 pixels. The ideal resolution is 400 × 400 pixels. The maximum file size is 10 megabytes. "If either height or width exceeds 20,000 pixels, your photo will not upload," according to LinkedIn.

Background Banner Image

This should be between 1,000 × 425 pixels and 4,000 × 4,000 pixels. Ideal size is 1,400 × 425 pixels. The maximum file size is 4 megabytes.

Character Limits

First name	20	Company name	100	Interests	1,000
Last name	40	Position title in experience section	100	Honors and awards	1,000
URL	5–30				
Headline	120			Advice for contacting	2,000
		Education	100		
Address	1,000	Position/ experience description	1,000	Project description	2,000
Website URL	256				
Website anchor text	30			Publication description	2,000
		Education description	1,000		
Summary	2,000				

Other Specifications/Limitations

Choose up to fifty skills.
Choose up to one hundred groups.

What to Avoid on LinkedIn (or "Be Careful")

Many of my students or audience members have a fear of making a mistake on LinkedIn. I see it every day. Mistakes do happen occasionally. Over the past decade while I have been enjoying LinkedIn, I have personally made a couple of these mistakes myself. This is my "be careful" list especially for you:

1. **Be selective**. Don't invite everyone in your database to connect. I know that LinkedIn promotes the feature of uploading (or syncing) your contacts, but I never recommend that action. Instead, select "skip" and add connections one at a time with a personal invitation and follow-up.
2. **Be savvy**. Try not to post or comment about religion or politics. It's certainly OK on your profile if you work for a campaign, church, or synagogue but be very careful about posting specific political or religious views. You wouldn't start a business meeting talking about the upcoming campaign, so it's really the same kind of thing.
3. **Be positive**. Always be positive and helpful on LinkedIn. LinkedIn is not the place for criticism or complaints. If you have to message someone with an issue, send a private InMail message. Some companies have Twitter accounts set up for customer service, so that would be a more appropriate place to lodge your complaint.
4. **Be professional**. Don't share family or overly personal photos, stories, or updates (e.g., family Christmas photos, fraternity party photos, or photos of the big fish you caught; these are all great for Facebook). Write about your personal interests and family in the "interests" part of your profile. That's it. Your posts, shares, and comments should be professional and business oriented. If you see others posting

highly personal content, your best course of action is to ignore it. If the person is a good friend, you can privately share this best practice tip with him or her to be helpful.

5. **Be sensitive.** Don't over post. If you like and comment on everything, your network will likely tire of the noise. I am comfortable liking or sharing a couple of things per day on LinkedIn, but I try my best not to go overboard.

6. **Be brave.** Don't be scared to like or share other people's articles. Learn how to share content because it's a good way to connect with your network. If your company is sending content to you, it is highly unlikely you will make a mistake by sharing it with your network. Review the article first and then share, like, or comment. My favorite thing to share is a congratulations message for a friend who has won an award, written a book, or reached a major milestone.

7. **Be aware.** Understand what is private versus public within LinkedIn. Realize that when you like, share, or comment on a post, it is publicly viewable on the home feed of your network. Groups are now more private, but always assume eyes are on your posts. Everyone in the group will have access to your post. InMails, invitations, and job applications are private within the LinkedIn platform. Don't post your entire birthday on any social media site. I don't like birthdays on LinkedIn but some people do. If you decide to post your birthday, be sure to delete the year to avoid identity theft.

8. **Be creative.** Expand out of your comfort zone. Consider blogging on the LinkedIn Publisher platform or building a relationship with a person you identified in a LinkedIn Group. Expand your profile to truly incorporate your unique personal brand in the best possible light. The platform is here, so what are you waiting for?

9. **Be modest.** Don't be overtly selling or bragging. Use the same etiquette you would in real life scenarios. Use LinkedIn to build relationships and share expertise. Be the helpful expert and not the braggart. Demonstrate your passion and expertise on your complete profile, which reflects your unique personal brand.

10. **Be smart and be yourself.** Manage your profile and account actively. Have a great photo, headline, and summary that reflects your unique personal brand. Make sure your profile is 100 percent complete. Watch your grammar, spelling, and posts. Remove any duplicate profiles. Always follow LinkedIn's terms of service. The more you enjoy working on your brand and network, the more benefit you will derive out of the experience!

LinkedIn Premium Services

LinkedIn.com Platform—Free and Premium

The free features available on the LinkedIn platform include the following:

- LinkedIn profile
- first-level connections; build your network
- messaging (InMail) to your first-level connections
- ability to find and follow companies
- ability to read and share content
- ability to blog on the LinkedIn Publisher platform
- ability to join or create LinkedIn Groups
- ability to search for jobs
- ability to give and receive recommendations and endorsements
- ability to search for people and build your network

There are several premium versions of LinkedIn, including Personal Plus, Job Seeker, Business Plus, and Executive. All the premium versions offer a ninety-day view of "Who's Viewed Your Profile" and a few other features. The exact features vary by version and LinkedIn tends to change the capability sets. Additional features include the following:

- premium profile
- larger search listing
- seven search filters
- featured applicant—for Job Seeker
- applicant insights—for Job Seeker
- salary data—for Job Seeker
- InMail messages

Other LinkedIn premium services are on their own unique platforms; these include Recruiter and Sales Navigator, which are described below.

Recruiter Platform—for HR and Recruiting Pros

This is an advanced platform for recruiters to find candidates among the entire LinkedIn database. Recruiters may send InMail messages outside of their network. Recruiter also offers robust tracking, reporting, and visibility of profiles.

Sales Navigator Platform—for Sales Pros

This is an advanced platform for sales representatives. The service segments the people and companies that the sales rep is targeting for prospecting. InMails can be sent outside of the network. LinkedIn also provides additional company insights to Sales Navigator users and some advanced team features and reporting and a dashboard.

Resources for Appendix E

Register at the companion website (http://www.linkedinforpersonalbranding .com) for information on the following:

- LinkedIn Premium
- LinkedIn Premium FAQ

THANK YOU!

Thank you for joining me on this journey of personal branding with LinkedIn. I wish you huge success! I hope you found it very useful for your business and/or career.

If you found this book helpful or inspiring in any way, I hope you will take a moment to *write a short review*. Your help is greatly appreciated.

Please also consider joining my e-mail list to keep up to date with me, the book, and LinkedIn.

www.linkedinforpersonalbranding.com

Today's first impressions are happening on LinkedIn.

Is your LinkedIn presence helping you to advance your sales, recruiting, or career opportunities? Are you confident in your personal brand and LinkedIn profile? In LinkedIn for Personal Branding: The Ultimate Guide, Long shares how to uncover and present your unique brand and how to become a thought leader on LinkedIn. With numerous real examples and case studies, LinkedIn for Personal Branding: The Ultimate Guide is a must–read for today's current or aspiring professionals.

"Sandra Long's book, LinkedIn for Personal Branding, will be a 'go-to' resource I'll use when referring career seeking working professionals to valuable career tools!"

—Laurie Sedgwick
Director of Career Management, Executive MBA Programs & Alumni Support
Johnson School @ Cornell University

"Sandra Long provides you with a formula for success to grow, enhance and expand….Pick up a copy of her book to take your personal brand to the next level on LinkedIn."

- Jessica Miller-Merrell
Founder of Blogging4Jobs and Workology. Author of Tweet This! Twitter for Business

Sandra Long is an in-demand speaker, consultant, entrepreneur, and trainer working with corporations, universities, and individuals. She owns and manages Post Road Consulting LLC, a company that exclusively provides sales, talent and career solutions around the LinkedIn experience. Sandra is passionate about empowering her customers and readers by leveraging personal branding, professional etiquette and LinkedIn.

HybridGlobal
PUBLISHING

ISBN 978-1-938015-43-4
90000
9 781938 015434